Werner Biermann

Tanganyika Railways – Carrier of Colonialism

Afrikanische Studien

Band 9

LIT

Werner Biermann

Tanganyika Railways – Carrier of Colonialism

An Account of Economic Indicators and Social Fragments

LIT

Die Deutsche Bibliothek – CIP-Einheitsaufnahme

Biermann, Werner
Tanganyika Railways – Carrier of Colonialism : An Account of Economic Indicators and Social Fragments / Werner Biermann .
– Münster : Lit, 1995
   (Afrikanische Studien ; 9 .)
   ISBN 3-8258-2524-8

NE: GT

© LIT VERLAG
Dieckstr. 73   48145 Münster   Tel. 0251–23 50 91   Fax 0251–23 19 72

Contents

Preface/ Acknowledgments vi
Terminology vii
Abbreviations vii
Map viii

1 Introductory Remarks 1
2 Tanganyika under Colonialism 3
3 Railways in Tanganyika 23
4 Railway Organisation 43
5 Administration and Economic Policy 71
6 Work Place Reality 87
7 The Rise of Organised Protest 117
8 Conclusion 141

Bibliography 143

Preface/ Acknowledgments

The research for this book was influenced by various sources. John Campbell, Swansea, and Haroub Othman, Dar es Salaam, made valuable comments on colonialism in Tanganyika and the beginnings of wage labour relations. Above all, the access to John's unpublished material helped me clarify my ideas. I am very grateful to him.

At Paderborn, Arno Klönne encouraged my research from his wider focus on wage labour conditions and work place realities. It is intended to contribute to this focus with the history of wage labour in Tanzania in the near future. The present publication, therefore, is one study in this wider field which should help the understanding for one important work place in colonial Tanganyika.

Paderborn Werner Biermann
July 1995

Terminology

Currency: The East African shilling was equal in value to the British shilling. One shilling contained 100 cents. Twenty shillings (Shs.) made up one British pound. Until 1914, one German mark was equal in value to one shilling. The German East African rupee (Rs.) was equal to twenty marks, after the reform of 1905.

Distance: The metric system was adopted. One mile equals 1.6093 kilometres.

Weight: Based on the metric system. One ton avoirdupois is equivalent to 1.0160 metric tons.

Abbreviations

Chief Sec.	Chief Secretary
DSM	Dar es Salaam
E.A.R.H.	East African Railways and Harbours (1948 - 1969)
GMR	General Manager, Tanganyika Railways
K.U.R.	Kenya and Uganda Railways (1926 - 1948)
Lab. Com.	Labour Commissioner
LO	Labour Officer
Provincer	Provincial Commissioner
R.L.S.	Railways Local Service
RAA	Railway African Association
(Sub) PWI.	(Sub) Permanent Ways Inspector
TAA	Tanganyika African Association
TANU	Tanganyika African National Union
TFL	Tanganyika Federation of Labour
TNA	Tanzania National Archives
TR	Tanganyika Railways (1919 - 1948)
TSGA	Tanganyika Sisal Growers Association
UR	Uganda Railway (1896 - 1926)

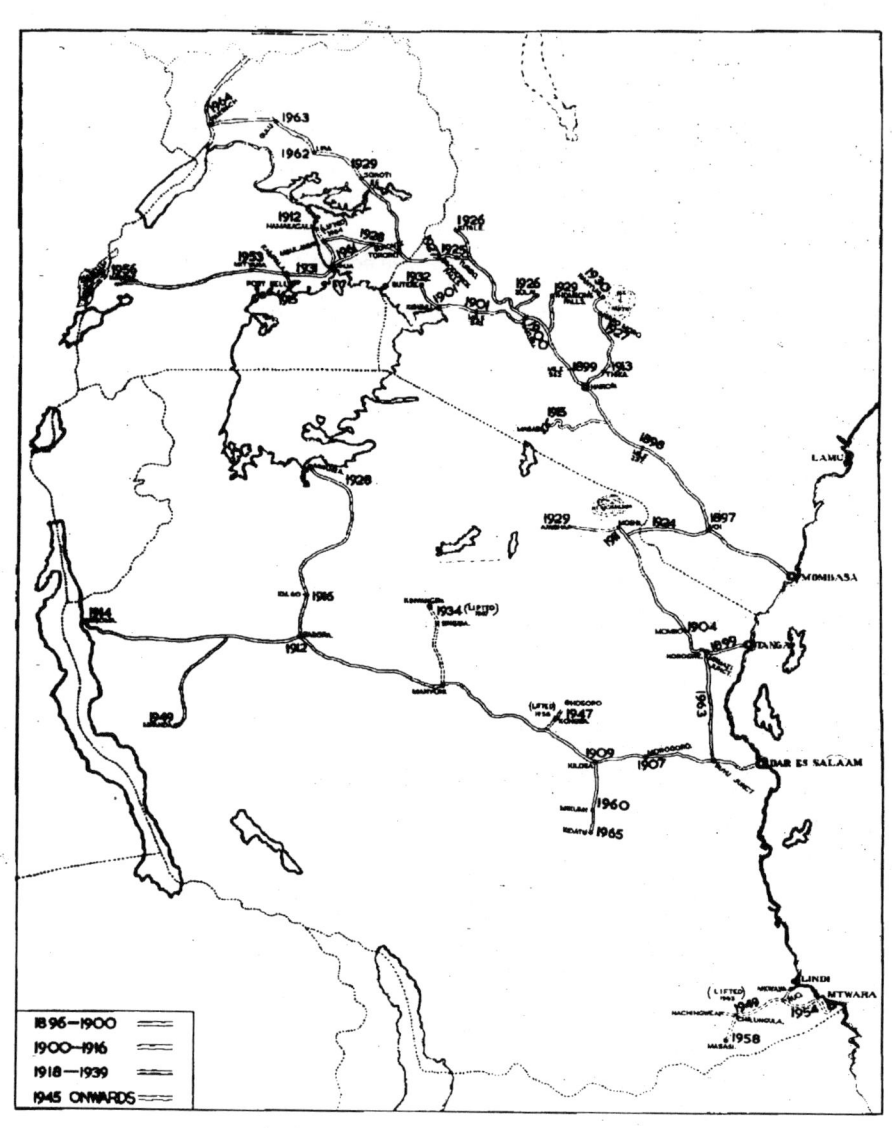

1. Introductory Remarks

Mechanisation of transport systems accompanied the first period of industrialisation. Obviously, railway systems formed the backbone of the colonial economies. In the industrialised core-nations the railways laid the foundations for an efficient infrastructure that connected markets and industries. However, in the colonial periphery the railways served one purpose, that is the cheapest transportation of exportable products. The existence of *Stichbahn* (branch terminal line) clearly portrays the economic system of colonialism - the unilateral transfer of resources for industrial growth in the core-nations.

Regarding Tanganyika the role of the railways under colonialism has not attracted academic attention. One reason must be looked after the availability of archival sources. Many German sources that document the construction of the Central Line seem to be unretrievable. Major archival material of the Tanganyika Railways (Secretarial File R. "Railways") was burned in 1951 and destroyed when after January 1954 the Secretariat Registry was decentralised with inadequate storage facilities at the old airport.[1] Another reason follows from the 'Tanzania debate' of the seventies that focused on socialist reconstruction. Although the railway "is still the backbone of the entire transport system [and] has very significantly influenced the present economic structure of the country"[2] this debate simply ignores it when discussing development strategies.[3] Railways, the most efficient mass transport system, declined in socialist Tanzania; measured against ton mileage the Tanzania

---

[1] Patricia J. Hill, *National Archives of Tanzania. Shelf List and Index to Secretariat Archives. Early Series (1919-1927)*. Dar es Salaam, February 1966; also Marcia Wright, *Report on the National Archives*. Dar es Salaam, 1962.
[2] Rolf Hofmeier, *Transport and Economic Development in Tanzania with particular reference to roads and road transport*. München, 1972, pp.240f.
[3] See inter alia Kwan S. Kim et al. (ed.), *Papers on the Political Economy of Tanzania*. Nairobi, 1979; Lionel Cliffe and John S. Saul (ed.), *Socialism in Tanzania. An Interdisciplinary Reader. Vol.1 Politics. Vol. 2 Policies*. Nairobi, 1973; and Bismarck U. Mwansasu and Cranford Pratt (ed.), *Towards Socialism in Tanzania*. Dar es Salaam, 1979.

Railway Corporation showed poorer results than its colonial predecessor in spite of the sustained growth of the economy.[4]

In particular, these reasons form what the French call 'la scène de séduction'. The present publication contributes to the restoration of one important factor in Tanzania's colonial past. For the afore-mentioned objective constraints the following presentation remains an approach with a specific mould. The railways are placed in the broader context of colonialism what identifies their economic and social role.

Therefore, the introductory chapter discusses the general trends of colonialism in Tanganyika to be followed from the history of the railway system. Against the general background the next chapter presents the organisational structure of the Tanganyika Railways that leads to the economic analysis. It will be shown that the Railways was forced into the financial policy of 'credit peonage' that immediately blocked the modernisation of infrastructure and equipment, and founded the employment policy of labour-intensive works and cheap African labour. For financial objectives the African work force was denied any form of organisation that rendered the Railways the features of the typical colonial enterprise. This pattern explains why workers' demands for adequate pay and job security were linked to strikes and spontaneous protests what will be discussed in the chapters on 'Work Place Reality' and 'Organised Protest'.

Finally, from a development position the Railways contributed nothing to industrial stimulation because locomotives, rolling stock, and other equipment were imported from Britain. Indeed, railway policy should be approached from state-financed incentives for metropolitan capital-goods industries.[5] This observation gives additional support to the classification of the Tanganyika Railways as " Carrier of Colonialism".

---

[4] Bank of Tanzania, *Tanzania: Twenty Years of Independence (1961-1981). A Review of Political and Economic Performance.* Dar es Salaam, n.d., p.147.
[5] Ralph A. Austen, *African Economic History. Internal Development and External Dependency.* London, 1987, p.128.

2. Tanganyika under Colonialism

How deeply colonial politics effected the traditional societies in Tanzania and how devastating German rule in that part of Africa might have been, colonialism did not stop at that point but translated into far-reaching change of the previously established political economy. This translation proved in i) the destruction of the long-distance trade network; ii) the introduction of capitalistic regulations, such as the commoditisation of land, wage labour, and taxation; and iii) the ecological disaster in the wake of colonial wars and politics of domination. These aspects deserve a closer examination for two reasons: the understanding of colonial induced pillage and devastation, and the rise of railway systems after the destruction of the efficient, porter-based trade network.

I.

The destruction of the long-distance trade system followed colonial occupation. On the one hand, the German army was employed to impose the colonial power's political dictate on Tanzanian societies that resisted the loss of autonomy. On the other hand, the partition of East Africa among the European powers separated Zanzibar, the commercial centre, from the mainland while the Belgian conquest of the Congo deprived the traditional merchant capital from its major source of ivory supply. Zanzibar itself, against which Britain had previously launched massive attacks aimed at the abolition of slavery, now became the social laboratory where British officials set out to implant their ideas of a modern, post-slavery society. Geopolitics combined with economics of colonialism, and these factors destroyed the former commercial engine that had propelled East Africa: Ivory the staple product of the nineteenth century became a trophy for wealthy tourists[6] summarise this economic transformation whose magnitude is reflected by official trade figures. In 1913, the ivory trade

---

[6] John Iliffe, *A Modern History of Tanganyika*. Cambridge, 1979, p.130.

equalled 0.6 per cent of the Tanganyika exports and amounted to 230,000 marks whereas at the eve of the partition ivory exports had reached approximately 4,000,000 marks.[7]

Control of the Tanganyika coast was of eminent importance in German strategic designs;[8] while Britain acknowledged the German advance even though it contradicted the 1885 agreements.[9] The Zanzibar sultanate lacked vigour and political commitment to resist the German occupation of the coast. Opposition emerged from the freshly conquered - the Abushiri uprising united the commercial and land-owning classes precisely because of the colonial degrees of taxation and land alienation.[10] It rapidly translated into a mass movement as the Germans ignored Islamic laws and customs that they substituted by their social regulations whose rationale must eclipse the coastal people. During the first months of the uprising the Germans suffered a series of military defeats documented by the re-conquest of the major coastal towns: Bagamoyo, Pangani in the north; Kilwa, Lindi and Mikindani farther south. The reasons that spared the supposedly most efficient European army from surrender and gradually shifted the military balance to the colonial power have to be looked into the sociological composition of the uprising.[11]

The commercial rivalry among merchant capitalists had gathered momentum in the 1850s. The political masters of the East African emporium, the Omanis preserved the commercial monopoly at the Mrima coast, the traditional name of the Tanganyika coast-line, against European and American competition whose companies domina-

---

[7] Ivory trade declined dramatically for two reasons. The colonial partition resulted into new colonial states which were oriented at the respective metropolitan economies while former inter-regional spheres of exchange were abolished. In the case of ivory, the new isolation jeopardised the Tanganyika trade particularly because of the depletion of elephant herds in western Tanganyika.
[8] German colonialism in Africa originated from a side-effect of Bismarck's sophisticated and - with hindsight's clarity - masterly orchestrated diplomacy in a much wider game. This explains the lack of ambition once the diplomatic objectives were achieved. But it also contributed to chauvinist currents connected with colonialism which, in the post-Bismarck period, gave support to the political maze. It now appeared that the African colonies could be exploited for geo-political ambitions - the 'Mittelafrika-Konzept' through which British hegemony should be challenged. In addition, the access to the Katangese raw materials was another reason for the railway construction in Tanganyika; cf. H.Ulrich Wehler, *Bismarck und der Imperialismus*. Köln, 1972, pp.354-5.
[9] For Germany's strategy see George Hallgarten, *Imperialismus vor 1914. Die soziologischen Grundlagen der Außenpolitik europäischer Großmächte vor dem Ersten Weltkrieg*. Erster Band, München, 1963, p.352. The British policy is summarised by Thomas Pakenham, *The Scramble for Africa 1876-1912*. London, 1991, pp.297-315.
[10] On the Abushiri uprising see J.A. Kiernan, 'Abushiri and the Germans', *Hadith 2*, 1970, pp.157-201; for the wider context of resistance against colonial conquest see G.C.K. Gwassa, 'The German intervention and African resistance in Tanzania', in I.N. and A.J. Temu (ed.), *A history of Tanzania*. Nairobi, 1969, pp.85-122.
[11] For more details see Werner Biermann, *Wachuurizi Na Halasa. Händler und Handelskapital in der wirtschaftlichen Entwicklung Ostafrikas (900 bis 1890)*. Münster und Hamburg, 1993, pp.205-276.

ted the Zanzibar entrepot. One decade later the Mrima coast experienced the second capital movement. This time, Omani planters and their Indian financiers identified geographical diversification as only alternative against the anti-slavery legislation which Britain, the informal master of East Africa, had imposed on the Omani lords. For tactical reasons and political commitment elsewhere Britain, at least for the moment, abstained from extending the abolition laws to the East African mainland. The slave-run clove and coconut plantations, Zanzibar's economic backbone next to the ivory trade, faced a structural crisis once the slave labour supply was blocked to what added the self-inflicted depressed clove world market. The Omani producers expanded production regardless of the stagnant demand. Thus, since the early 1850s prices declined and curtailed the planters' profits who were forced into massive borrowing from Indian financiers. Profit squeeze and debt trap summarise the situation; it also explains the spread of investment at the Mrima coast. Obviously, merchants and planters showed vested interests in defending their economic privileges against the colonial invaders.

Abushiri, the leader of the uprising and member of the planter élite, clearly saw - what hindsight's wisdom suggests - that mass support was needed if resistance was successful.[12] Besides mere tactical requirements, Abushiri identified the political paralysis of Zanzibar and consequently orientated the anti-colonial struggle not at the restoration of the old political order but embarked on a more ambitious scheme - the Mrima independence.

Mass backing was needed simply because the future socio-economic matrix pointed towards a peasant-based society instead of the slave-holding system. Understandably therefore that the ruling families, the *waungwawa*, resisted this scheme. Open conflict occurred immediately after the early defeat of the German troops, a success that was mainly owed to run-away slaves whom Abushiri granted free-citizen status. Due to these conflicts the uprising lost its momentum, and what counted even more, the leadership had to abandon the former guerrilla strategy. In conventional warfare the colonial army proved its superiority with tactic and *materiel*; supported from a British naval squadron and freshly recruited troops dispatched to the East African theatre the Germans restored control and drove Abushiri into sur-

---

[12] For the following see J. Glassman, 'Social Rebellion and Swahili Culture: The Response to German Conquest of the Northern Mrima, 1888-1890.' Ph.D.thesis, University of Wisconsin, 1988, pp.481ff.; R.D. Jackson, 'Resistance to the German invasion', in Robert I. Rotberg and A.A. Mazrui (ed.), *Protest and Power in Black Africa*. New York, 1970, pp.51, 55-6.

render. After one year's fight the uprising collapsed. The coastal towns, the terminals of the nineteenth century long-distance trade, lost control over the trade and degenerated into impoverished posts - a process that was rapidly completed thanks to the military zeal with which German colonialism achieved the command over the hinterland.[13]

The central caravan route that connected the Congolese Manyema by way of Tabora, the main staple post, with coastal Bagamoyo from where ivory, and at a later stage slaves, was shipped to Zanzibar was annihilated. After the conquest of the Wagogo, go-betweens in the trade, Unyamwezi, the magnet of the trade, became the next target. Again, the Germans suffered an early defeat due to the military and political skill of Iseke, successor to the legendary Mirambo, the founder of the Wanyamwezi commercial state. In military terms, the African troops outwitted the conventionally drilled European officers and *askaris* (African mercenaries) who were forced into retreat. Similar to the Abushiri uprising social conflicts came to the colonial power's rescue. Iseke's strength stemmed from his pro-peasant policy. Taxing the Wanyamwezi merchant class, *wandewa*, enabled him to surplus redistribution in favour of the peasantry. Opposition combined the *wandewa* with local chiefs, *ntemi*, who feared the loss of privileges. A populist leader like Iseke automatically threatened the former fabric of influence and hierarchy and thus, the alliance with the Germans promised a solution against the social and political erosion. The quest for the status quo blinded *ntemi* and *wandewa* against the real motives of the colonialists who too willingly accepted the opposition's demand as it changed the military balance into their favour. Thus, Iseke's fate was sealed as was the opposition's some years later.

The Germans entirely ignored their allies' demand and obliged the newly enthroned *ntemi*, Nyaso, to recruit porters and workers for the coastal plantations. Obviously, collaboration was not what Nyaso had dreamt of. Moreover, the merchant class was quickly degraded as well and forced into compulsory labour. The inevitable resistance, however, was short-lived as it lacked mass support. The common Wanyamwezi found it difficult to join the former masters while, on the other hand, the colonial economy initiated social change. The Wanyamwezi had previously supplied the caravans with porters. The magnitude of portage work affected the social com-

---

[13] The following account is based on Kurt Büttner, *Die Anfänge der deutschen Kolonialpolitik in Ostafrika. Eine kritische Untersuchung an Hand unveröffentlichter Quellen.* Berlin, 1959, p.90. For the military aspects in German colonial conquest see H. von Bülow, *Deutschlands Kolonien und Kolonialkriege.* Leipzig, 1900, pp.71-148.

position as a new social class emerged whose reproduction was entirely orientated at paid work - a historical rupture for a peasant society. This working class in the making followed its specific goals which were barely compatible with the traditional social values. As modern men, these porters faced new challenges in the wake of the colonial economy what absorbed their energies. The social conditions and wage ceiling on the coastal plantations became more important than the quest of power by traditional authorities.

The long-distance trade system was the most spectacular and probably the most rewarding of similar exchange systems on regional level. It is misleading to approach nineteenth century East African economics solely from long-distance trade. The emergence of commercialised surplus exchange cast that century into its historical mould which in combination with social change and political transformation from mystified rule into territorial states indicated the beginning of modernity in East Africa. This change was propelled by and rested upon commerce as the latter enabled the augmentation of surplus generation. Surplus enlarged translated into the recompensation of the social matrix along new class lines - henceforth, economics started to define the social formation.

An average caravan comprised more than 1,000 people; at the height of the trade at least 20 to 30 caravans were on the march to or from the coast. For obvious reasons, the caravans must fall back on local food supplies simply as i) the carrying of food would curtail the caravan's commercial capacity while ii) one person is incapable of transporting the total amount of his food supplies for the approximately three months march from the coast to Unyamwezi. Physical constraints made the reliance on local sources inevitable to what added the political constellation as societies through whose territories the caravans passed extracted toll in exchange for protection. The caravans were thus obliged to carry exchangeable goods which formed the basis of inter-regional exchanges what, finally, resulted into specialisation and differentiation even among the societies with indirect access to the long-distance trade network.[14] The exchange system was still in its early stage when the colonial attack started. This classification helps to understand why the system rapid-

---

[14] Based on R.W. Beachey, 'East African Ivory Trade in the Nineteenth Century', *Journal of African History*, 2, 8, 1967, p.271; Norman R. Bennett, 'Arab Impact', in Bethwell A. Ogot (ed.), *Zamani. A Survey of East African History*. Nairobi, 1974, p.216, and Beverly Brown, 'Ujiji: The History of a Lakeside Town, c.1800-1914.' Ph.D.thesis, Boston University, 1973, pp.38-86.

ly disappeared followed by disorientation and disarray particularly because of the economic inconsistencies which surprisingly featured German colonialism.

II.

Inconsistencies comprise two closely interwoven elements: the colonial power's obvious disdain against the continuity of the ivory trade regardless of the economic potentials and its difficulties to translate the productive forces having previously been tied to this trade into capital accumulation. These observations point towards the immanent conflicts of German colonialism, i.e., the quest for an economically powerful colony while relying on the 'settler factor' instead of corporate capital which abstained from colonial investment in East Africa as elsewhere. Before taking up this issue the second pole of the long-distance trade, the Zanzibar entrepôt, requires detailed analysis.

German aggression, launched by private adventurers and later backed by the imperial state, altered the East African balance of power, a balance which portrayed the subtle control by Great Britain over a region whose relevance stemmed from geopolitical concerns about India, the second pillar of the British global hegemony. A commercial empire, Zanzibar orientated itself at economics but abstained from territorial annexation of the African mainland. Nevertheless, this low political profile neither shielded Zanzibar against great power clashes nor did the abolition laws having been introduced under British pressure pay for strategic support once German aggression gathered momentum. The Zanzibar sultanate after 1885 learnt the lesson of dependency.[15] Until 1890, it was not only denied its political sovereignty, its sphere of influence on the coast and the hinterland but also suffered from British intervention which ended the island's economic fabric. In formal terms a protectorate since 1890, Zanzibar, in essence, was controlled by Britain. Control translated into economics of plunder and agrarian reform. Being highly successful with the former Britain, however, failed to implant agrarian capitalism.

Firstly, Britain forced Zanzibar into compensation payments for the collapsed *Imperial British East Africa Company*. The legal position remained highly questionable

---

[15] For the following see Norman R. Bennett, *A History of the Arab State of Zanzibar*. London, 1978, pp.187-8, 189-91, 218-9; J. Flint, 'Zanzibar 1890-1950', in V. Harlow and E.M. Chilver (ed.), *History of East Africa*. Vol. II. Nairobi, 1982, pp.647-8,

and outspokenly dubious but it helped to safeguard government against parliamentary inquiries into what seemed to become another colonial *chronique scandaleuse*. The sum of £200,000 equalled the compensation payment which Germany had paid the sultan in return for territorial concessions at the Mrima coast.

Secondly, British intention combined free wage labour with the improvement of the island's ailing plantation economy. Under the Anti-Slavery Decree of August 1890 buying and selling of slaves became illegal while the slaves were granted the right of emancipation. Both measures undermined the plantations which already suffered from indebtedness and inefficiency.[16] According to Victorian ethics, 'hard work' was recognised to be the sole means to reset deprived social classes on the path of civic virtues. The grand scheme failed in Zanzibar primarily because of tactical concerns. At the height of the pre-war arms race Britain lacked the funds for this scheme which subsequently justified alliances with the Zanzibar planter class: preservation of the political status quo prevailed over ambitious reforms whose impact was shouldered on the former slaves. Instead of emancipation, the *wazalia* (freed slaves) emerged as squatters. In exchange for land the squatters worked on the plantations notably during the peak harvest season. Routine work became the realm of migrant labour from Tanganyika mainland mainly from Unyamwezi. Whereas the ivory collapsed the clove production resumed prosperity thanks to the economic policy backing viz. wage and rent regulations, infrastructure support and debt rescheduling.

As for the last aspect, colonial administration took over from private, mainly Indian creditors and adjusted credits and repayments to the economic potentials of the plantation sector. In return, the planters agreed on modern agro-techniques with cloves being marketed under government auspices.

Apart from voluntary migrant labour the Zanzibar plantation economy cut the links with the African mainland whereas the island's former role of entrepôt underwent the gradual change from staging post to backwater. In the early colonial days Zanzibar served German Tanganyika which i) lacked sophisticated harbour facilities while ii) for the same reason the major trading companies preferred the island.[17] Therefore, roughly 50 per cent of Tanganyika's foreign trades went through this port. At the sa-

---

[16] Frederick Cooper, *From Slaves to Squatters. Plantation Labour and Agriculture in Zanzibar and Coastal Kenya, 1890-1925*. Nairobi, 1981, pp.75-6, 84-7, 90-2.
[17] For the history and development of East Africa's harbours see inter alia B.S. Hoyle, 'Early Port Development in East Africa', *Tijdschrift voor Economische en Sociale Geograpfie*, LVIII, 1967.

me time, Zanzibar served in a similar function for British East Africa, i.e., Kenya and the Uganda Protectorate.

In both cases the railways announced the withdrawal of traffic and capital - the completion of the Uganda railway founded Mombasa's prominence simply because the shipment of the colonial produce necessitated an efficient harbour. The same, although on a minor scale, referred to Tanga and Dar es Salaam, the terminals of the 'Nordbahn' and the 'Mittellandbahn' (Central Line), respectively. Henceforth, East Africa's world trade was handled by the coastal ports and Zanzibar lost its former dominance. Even worse, it was via Mombasa that the island's foreign trades were handled. The step into a trade backwater is evidenced by empirical proof. At the eve of the first world war, Zanzibar port was in charge of less than 10 per cent of the East African cargo.[18] Indeed, the former trade network was terminated.

In the light of the DOAG's (Deutsche Ostafrika Gesellschaft) precarious finances and the reluctance of metropolitan monopolies of investing into the colony the destruction of the long-distance trade was negative as it diminished the stock of extractable revenues. The structural advantages of abundant and proletarianised labour and weakened peasantry became economic assets if and when activated by capital injections. And precisely at this point the weaknesses of German colonialism were evident.

Colonialism originated from great power diplomacy whose relevance diminished in proportion to new political challenges such as the quest for *Weltmacht* which predominated German politics after Bismarck's demise. In the wake of the 1890s arms race the big banks and industrial capital found more lucrative investment outlets in the metropolitan area than in the colonies.[19] This constellation reasoned the emergence of adventurer and settler capital in Tanganyika which neatly corresponded with the social forces who supported the 'Kolonialfrage' in imperial Germany. It also explains why atrocity continued after subjugation - the colonial administration, on the

---

[18] For reasons of economies the major shipping lines identified Zanzibar as their central entrepôt. Only at alter stage did the Imperial government mobilise funds for port modernisation. However, neither Dar es Salaam nor Tanga were equipped with deep-water berths, and cargoes were landed by lighters. In point of fact, the Imperial government subsidised the German East Africa Shipping Line which, after 1902/3, broke the Zanzibar-British East Africa trade monopoly over the colony and captured approximately two thirds of East Africa's exports by 1909; see W.O. Henderson,'German East Africa, 1884-1918', in V. Harlow and E.M. Chilver (ed.), *History of East Africa*. Vol. II. Nairobi, 1982, pp.123-62. According to the same source, the annual shipping subsidy amounted to £67,000 or 800,000 marks.

[19] Colonial investments equalled less than 4 per cent of total German foreign investment (direct and portfolio investments); the total investment stock in the colonies in 1914 amounted to c.600 million marks of which c. 85 million marks originated from German companies; cf. K. Most, *Die wirtschaftliche Entwicklung Deutsch-Ostafrikas, 1885-1905*. Berlin, 1905, passim.

one hand, and colonial capitalism, on the other, lacked the capital stock which might have allowed for adequate wages and work conditions. Because of the miserable conditions at the work place misery potential labour recruits were reluctant to identify capitalism as alternative to peasant poverty which, in turn, was further aggravated in order to meet i) the administration's financial requirements and ii) the labour demand of the capitalist sector. These factors produced the permanent state intervention particularly with regard to labour supplies to be organised by state agencies. It goes without saying that the state in matters of wage rates and legal positions fully backed the settlers and colonial capitalism in general.

Regardless of these interventions colonialism's economic profile remained poor, and thus, a self-propelled process of immiserisation started which victimised the peasant economy as well as colonial capitalism and cast the colonial economy into the particular mould of economic coercion and economic poverty.

At first sight, the enigma of permanent labour shortage in spite of the economically feeble colonialism is surprising: why did colonialism fail to cover the labour demand of its 606 plantations and 276 settler farms, a total acreage of 107,000 ha, from an indigenous population of approximately 7,5 million? Demography, however, reveals that the Germans were highly successful given that the total recruitable male work force comprised c. 800,000. In 1913, approximately 172,00 qualified as permanent wage labourers to what added the seasonal peak demand. Therefore, the annual work force exceeded 200,000 and equalled more than a quarter of the adult male population. This transfer imposed a heavy toll on the peasant reproduction nexus while, at the same time, it barely sufficed to put the capitalist ventures on a sound footing let alone the activation of the dormant potentials.

According to official reports only 19 per cent of the land formally occupied by settlers and plantation companies was used, or 107,000 ha out of 550,000 ha.[20] This constellation reflects on the above-defined process of immiserisation: colonial capitalism lacked the funds for efficient accumulation the basis of which depended on surplus extraction - revenue and labour - from the African peasantry who, in turn, resisted real subsumption, in Marx' terminology, because of the depressing possibilities for wage labour. Colonial capitalism, on the other hand, remained undeveloped because of the limited resources while access to metropolitan financing was preclu-

---

[20] In 1912, c. 81,000 ha were under cultivation of which rubber accounted for 32,000 ha. In the same year, more than 50,000 ha were transferred and/or auctioned according to Amtliche Jahresberichte des Reichskolonialamtes, 1913, III, pp.66-84.

ded for the same reason. In short, colonial capitalism remained encapsulated in the 'pre-take-off stage'.

By the outbreak of the world war the economy of German East Africa, and indeed of Germany's other colonies, was just beginning to be welded into a form useful to metropolitan capital and German *Weltpolitik*. The colony's exports had trebled between 1903 and 1910;[21] but colonial trade itself only constituted less than one per cent of all of the Reich's foreign trades.[22]

The rudiments of a labour market were taking shape but, given the failure of the capitalist sector to fully integrate the peasantry into the plantations, it depended crucially upon continued use of coercion. Taxation, pernicious forms of recruitment, depressed wages and various other techniques to extort labour were reinforced through the administration of colonial justice: between 1901 and 1913 64,600 Africans were sentenced to corporal punishment, an average of five a week at every district office.[23] Despite administrative reforms and the introduction of supposedly pro-African labour legislation restricting some recruiting abuses, in 1911-2 a minimum of 5,944 official floggings were given. Further, in the same year courts and/or district officers sentenced 16 Africans to death, imprisoned 11,845, and fined 3,518 individuals. The vast majority of sentences were labour-related offences, e.g., abscondment, insubordination, etc. and underlined in no uncertain terms the political cum class dimension inherent in the administration of 'justice'.[24]

The institutionalisation of authority under the colonial administration and away from individual administrative officers must also have had an impact on the slender basis of legitimacy given German rule by what Iliffe has called the system of 'local compromises'.[25] Instrumental in establishing a minimal basis for local administration in the '90s, this system of compromises was essentially an ad hoc personal arrangement between individual field officers and the local factions/ cliques which officers recognised by investing with a semblance of authority.[26] This system broke down by 1905, in part because of stress caused by the outbreak of the Maji Maji rebellion, but more so because such arrangements lacked legitimacy in the eyes of the dominated

---

[21] To 20.8 million marks and equalled 27 per cent of the total exports from Germany's African colonies. A large proportion of Tanganyika exports went to India and England.
[22] L.H. Gann and P. Duignan, *The Rulers of German Africa, 1884-1914*. London, 1975, pp.248, 218.
[23] Iliffe, Modern History of Tanganyika, p.150.
[24] Gann and Duignan, Rulers of German Africa, pp.102-3.
[25] John Iliffe, *Tanganyika Under German Rule 1905-1912*. Cambridge, 1969, ch.7.
[26] K.W. von Sperber, *Public Administration in Tanzania*. München, 1970, pp.19f.

societies. Invested with authority and power not born of traditional leadership norms, such personalistic ad hoc measures could not withstand the strains which African societies were being increasingly subject to, their collapse was inevitable.[27]

The attempt by Governor Rechenberg to centralise the administration together with the upheavals taking place in African societies seem to indicate that, rather than a period of compromise followed by the 'politics of improvement', it would be more useful to talk of this period as an intermediate stage in peasant integration into the world market, itself one level of the transition from direct colonial domination towards effective civilian administration.[28]

The history of German occupation in East Africa should therefore be perceived as the result of the consistent application of a policy to exploit "the latent resources of the territory by whatever means came to hand".[29] The control exercised by the colonial administration over this process shifted to a more systematised form of 'ruling indirectly', but in reality the 'sphere of direct action' was simply political expedience tied to the interests of metropolitan capital. Evidence for this conclusion is amply provided in the unfettered role assumed by concessionaire and finance capital in the colony as against controls exercised over the settlers, on the one hand, and the build-up of a massive public debt to finance railroad construction by taxing Africans, on the other.

In the imperial scheme, it seemed to matter little that the colony was never able to absorb large numbers of settlers, indeed as Henderson has remarked, "[T]he more obvious it became that the colonies were of little use from the point of view of settlement the greater was the stress laid on their commercial value".[30]

And by the time it became clear that the colonies were not the commercial answer to the Reich's needs, indeed could not even meet their own expenses, wider politico-strategic considerations superseded economic calculations.

---

[27] See R.F. Eberlie, 'The German Achievement in East Africa', *Tanganyika Notes and Records*, 55, 1960, pp.190-2.
[28] Iliffe, Tanganyika Under German Rule, ch.5 and 6.
[29] Kenneth Ingham, *A History of East Africa*. London, 1965, p.193.
[30] Henderson, 'German East Africa, 1884-1918', p.45.

III.

Britain succeeded German colonialism in the administration of the Tanganyika territory. Tanganyika under the British Mandate was the second beginning due to impact, effect, and outcome of the war in East Africa, a secondary theatre of the world war but one of primordinary significance for the East African peoples. The *Kleinkrieg* devastated the country, its human and economic resources.[31] Reconstruction after the armistice faced a destroyed modern infrastructure while the African population, faminised by the guerrilla warfare, suffered from diseases. On top of that, the British mandatory power had to re-organise the ownership relations at the plantations and the settler farms.[32]

The objectives which guided British policy in Tanganyika stemmed from world political concerns and the financial constraints of metropolitan Britain. The pre-eminence of world political considerations in British colonialism in the inter-war period founded the mandatory status under the League of Nations. The search of financial consolidation and the economic constraints help to understand that colonial capitalism in Tanganyika was reproduced at a very low level with the emphasis of peasant producers, the carriers of financial surplus in British designs.[33]

The League of Nations, a supra-national forum, set out a new international order which should avoid new zones of conflicts and friction after the dismantling of the German, Austrian and Ottoman empires.[34]

As regards Tanganyika Britain administered the colony on behalf of the League of Nations.[35] The mandatory scheme regulated the gradual emancipation of the indigenous peoples and the development of free political institutions.[36] The constitutional charter provided for democratisation even though the concerned peoples were not asked about their positions.[37]

---

[31] About the war see B. Gardner, *German East. The Story of the First World War in East Africa*. London 1963, passim.
[32] According to J. Listowel, *The Making of Tanganyika*. London, 1965, p.67.
[33] See Werner Biermann, *Kolonie und City. Britische Wirtschaftsstrategie und -politik in Tanganyika, 1920-1955*. Saarbrücken and Fort Lauderdale, 1991, pp.5-10 for a more detailed account.
[34] For the League of Nations see inter alia A.P. Thornton, *Imperialism in the Twentieth Century*. London, 1980, pp.162, 184.
[35] See T.O. Lloyd, *The British Empire 1558-1983*. London, 1984, p.279.
[36] B.T.G. Chidzero, *Tanganyika and International Trusteeship*. Oxford, 1961, pp.263-8 on the Article vi of the Trusteeship Agreement.
[37] Listowel, Making of Tanganyika, p.66.

Tanganyika was administered from the Colonial Office which submitted its annual reports to the League's Permanent Mandates Commission.[38] The Commission lacked any power for influencing the mandatory power's policy and decision-making.[39]

Eventually, Britain's pragmatism prevailed over the legal superstructure as Tanganyika was fully incorporated into the wider planning of the East African Federation.[40] In other words, Tanganyika was turned into another British colony.

In July 1920, the Tanganyika Territory was formally established by the Tanganyika Order in Council.[41] The new administration faced immediate problems which followed from the devastation having been caused by the guerrilla-warfare.[42] The quest for recovery dictated the early colonial policy which, for the time being, preserved the German system of local administration. The akidas system[43] promised the dissemination of colonial authority and secured the collection of hut and poll taxes. Because of limited financial support from Great Britain the local taxes were elementary for the colonial budget.[44] The grants by the Imperial Treasury amounted to £400,000 while a £3 million loan was raised on the London financial market.[45] The capital injection was insufficient for infrastructure recovery what negatively affected the restoration of colonial capitalism. It follows that colonial administration had to focus on smallholder production for revenues.[46] Eventually, colonial strategy of Indirect Rule was designed along this line.

The German system of akidas only worked if propped up by the colonial army and an extended administration which for financial reasons was not feasible. Furthermore, the League of Nations' covenant requested the mandatory power to preparing the colonialised peoples for self-government. The British design focused on the existing

---

[38] John Hatch, *Tanzania. A Profile*. London, 1972, p.85.
[39] Kenneth Ingham, 'Tanganyika: The Mandate and Cameron, 1919-1931', in V. Harlow and E.M. Chilver (ed.), *History of East Africa*. Vol. II. Nairobi, 1982, p.546.
[40] Chidzero, Tanganyika and International Trusteeship, p.61.
[41] Ingham, 'Tanganyika: The Mandate and Cameron', p.550.
[42] Cf. Walter Rodney, 'The political economy of Tanganyika 1890-1930', in M.H.Y. Kaniki (ed.), *Tanzania under Colonial Rule*. London, 1980, p.143.
[43] Originally an adjunct of Arab rule over coastal and trading communities, the akidas occupied an intermediate position intended only in the very loose sense to administer on behalf of a central authority; their superior, the Sultan of Zanzibar, had not exercised any real authority over them or their communities. German occupation resurrected this institution and, after the extirpation of Arabs on the coast, gave it a central role in local administration that it had never before possessed. Transformed into native officials, akidas were given local responsibility for administration of justice, organising necessary labour supplies, and organising and overseeing compulsory agricultural production schemes.
[44] Listowel, Making of Tanganyika, p.71.
[45] Ingham, 'Tanganyika: The Mandate and Cameron', p.559. This loan was borrowed at normal market conditions because the Tanganyika Mandate did not qualify for preferential colonial loans; see Sidney Armitage-Smith, 'Report on a Financial Mission to Tanganyika, 26th September 1932'. *Cmd 4182*. London, 1932, passim.
[46] Ingham, 'Tanganyika: The Mandate and Cameron', p.551.

traditional institutions which should be recovered. It was assumed that the shocks of modernity could be evaded. The evolutionary approach implied a subtle monitoring of colonial development through which irritations and uncontrollable social processes might be dodged.[47]

Colonialism in Tanganyika abstained from social transformation; instead, it preserved social structures whose surplus it tapped off.[48] Thus a colonial model took shape which shielded peasant societies against capitalist penetration that featured paternalistic elements. It also blocked extended capitalist accumulation.[49] The latter caused the weakness of the krypto-capitalist classes: Asian businessmen and European entrepreneurs so that the colonial state appeared as the sole agent for development.[50] For reasons of economic constraints and financial difficulties the colonial power lacked the resources for colonial development what resulted in the drastic restrictions for European settlement and settler colonialism. In short, Indirect Rule was closer to crisis management than to capitalistic valorisation.[51]

The administrative reforms were preceded from the centralisation of the hut and poll tax and the restoration of native authorities.[52] The Native Authority Ordinance of 1923 laid the ground for the reforms as the colonial state searched for a solution of the 'budget squeeze'. African taxation was the most relevant revenue whose overhead costs should be reduced by the new administrative system.[53] Tanganyika was distinguished in territorial and local governments with the former representing the colonial political monopoly.[54] Local governments were placed under Native Authorities in accordance with customary law. The respective Ordinance of 1926 substituted for the former regulations that included the abolition of the akadia system. Henceforth, these authorities were entrusted with tax collection and maintaining order.[55]

---

[47] See E.K. Lumley, *Forgotten Mandate. A British District Officer in Tanganyika*. London, 1976, p.14-20; H.W. Stephens, *The Political Transformation of Tanganyika: 1920-67*. New York, 1968, p.53.
[48] According to Edward A. Brett, *Colonialism and Underdevelopment in East Africa. The politics of economic change 1919-1939*. London, 1973, pp.217ff.
[49] Hatch, Tanzania, p.89.
[50] Stephens, Political Transformation of Tanganyika, p.41.
[51] Stephens, Political Transformation of Tanganyika, p.58.
[52] Tax collection is documented by the Report on ways of Augmenting Taxes, 1934.
[53] Stephens, Political Transformation of Tanganyika, p.43. Varying from Shs.15 for the Masai to Shs.45 for the Baha of the Kasulu District the tax and poll tax was also correlated with the commercial possibilities as in times of contracting trades the peasantry withheld its surplus production from the market. The Native Authorities bound to the local community rather than to the colonial government accepted the declining tax collection. The average tax collection equalled £1.4 million p.a. or Shs.6 for every African, children included. On the other hand, resident Europeans were hardly taxed; a one per cent incomes tax being introduced only in 1932; Armitage-Smith, 'Report on a Financial Mission', pp.18, 27.
[54] Colonial Office Report 1927, pp.94ff; in addition, a Legislative Council consulted the colonial administration; see Ingham, 'Tanganyika: The Mandate and Cameron', p.567.
[55] Ingham, 'Tanganyika: The Mandate and Cameron', p.573.

The system of Indirect Rule strengthened the chiefly institutions mainly through the monetary lever as the rebate was increased to one third of the entire revenue in the early thirties. Out of this rebate some 68 percent were to pay the costs of tribal administration which included the salaries for the chiefs, their deputies and village headmen.[56] The system combined traditionalism to the requirements of the colonial state machinery in regards of revenue and monopoly of power.[57]

Traditionalism facilitated control as did the chiefly buffer stratum. Indirect Rule presented itself as the matrix of subtle suppression, an impasse which pointed neither towards a capitalist nor a pre-capitalist perspective.[58] Moreover, it aggravated the search of a solution in either direction because the Native Authority System sustained the dichotomy of traditional-local African spheres and the modern-territorial non-African spheres. Finally, the limited growth of social mobilisation helped to keep African perspectives confined to a very restricted scale.[59]

The absence of development incentives other than the reproduction of the patronising colonial model places macro-economic trends in the centre of analysis. Four phases can be distinguished; the first from 1919 to 1924 is classified as recovery period followed from a phase of boom and expansion which lasted until 1929. It came to a halt because of the world economic depression. Crisis lasted for three years. The following recovery came to an end by the outbreak of the second world war as the requirements of the British war economy led to the regrouping of economic activities in East Africa. The regional co-operation abolished the patronising model and led to 'modernisation by underdevelopment'.

By 1924 Tanganyika had recovered from the war damages.[60] The economic boom originated from the improved export performance that resulted in increased state revenues through customs and taxes.[61] The improved revenues rendered a sound foundation to the administrative apparatus and its linkages with the Native Authori-

---

[56] Colonial Office Report, 1931; J. Clagett Taylor, *The Political Development of Tanganyika*. Stanford, 1963, pp.49ff.
[57] In the words of one eminent eye-witness, Sir Charles Dundas, *African Crossroads*. London, 1955, pp.135ff.
[58] Hatch, Tanzania, pp.89-90.
[59] Stephens, Political Transformation of Tanganyika, p.57.
[60] Christine Leubuscher, *Tanganyika Territory. A Study of Economic Policy under Mandate*. Oxford, 1944, p.131.
[61] Exportations now averaged £ 4 million p.a.; a significant improvement against the £1.5 million annual average for the preceding years. Recurrent revenues averaged £1.7 million of which approximately two thirds originated from hut and poll tax; cf. Reports on Tanganyika Territory, 1928, p.26; 1933, p.42; Leubuscher, Tanganyika Territory, p.205, table C.1.

ties and also helped the repayments of Imperial loans.[62] Colonial administration spent almost 25 percent of revenues on loan repayments but barely invested in capital works such as infrastructure and public investments what outlines the paternalistic policy. To this adds the information that peasant production contributed almost £14 million to Tanganyika's foreign trades of £25.3 million for the years 1921 to 1931.[63] It becomes apparent that the tax squeeze met the colonial administration's main objective of balanced budgets.[64]

The shortcomings of this policy approach was felt during the economic depression. Depressed market prices caused peasant producers into the withdrawal from commercial relations.[65] Colonial revenues declined what aggravated the reproduction of the colonial model because the Native Authorities lost control over the communities.[66]

The predominance of foreign trades as factor of growth and basis of state revenues explains the economic damages of the global depression and the vexed mould of colonial policy. Even stricter economies were combined to higher taxation.[67] Financial consolidation also should qualify the colony for new credits.[68]

Depressed trades forced colonial administration into a two-fold strategy. The 'grow more crops campaign' aimed at the recovery of peasant production to be accompanied from the restructured distribution system. The former element focused on fair returns to the growers combined to quality controls whereas the latter envisioned state control through Native Authority Produce Markets, introduced in 1932.[69] Henceforth, all transactions were regulated on cash that eliminated petty Indian retailers, the former link between African peasants and the world market.[70] African cash crop producers, however, mobilised against the new Produce Markets whose activities were regarded as highly discriminatory: This was exemplified by the foundation of

---

[62] Recurrent surplus for the fiscal years 1925 to 1930 amounted to £1,407,000; Armitage-Smith, 'Report on a Financial Mission', p.36.
[63] Armitage-Smith, 'Report on a Financial Mission', p.9.
[64] Debt repayment instead of investment strangled the already curtailed prospects of capital accumulation, see Sally H. Frankel, *Capital Investment in Africa*. London, 1938, pp.276, 278.
[65] Market prices for cotton and groundnuts, the major peasant products, contracted by 50 percent and 43 percent between 1929 and 1931, respectively; see Leubuscher, Tanganyika Territory, p.204, table B.
[66] Revenue declined from £1,993,000 in 1929 to £1,522,000 two years later; a budget surplus of £205,000 turned into a deficit of £249,000; cf. Leubuscher, Tanganyika Territory, p.210, table D.1.
[67] Expenditure was cut by almost £500,000 what equals one third of the '29 budget; cf. Leubuscher, Tanganyika Territory, p.210, table D.1.
[68] Colonial Office Report, 1931, pp.20ff; Kenneth Ingham, 'Tanganyika: Slump and Short-term Governors, 1932-1945', V. Harlow and E.M. Chilver (ed.), *History of East Africa*. Vol. II. Nairobi, 1982.
[69] Leubuscher, Tanganyika Territory, p.51.
[70] The so-called bwana dukas had acted as middlemen for the British merchant houses in Dar es Salaam. During the crisis merchant capital reduced market prices for peasant products and, at the same time, increased import prices. The middlemen responded through barter trading which served the peasants as well.

the first co-operative society among the Kilimanjaro coffee growers. The attitude must be placed into the broader context of the rising African social opposition that outlined the incompatibility between colonial paternalism and the experience with colonial capitalism. Also, a change of colonial policy was felt whose concretisation was delayed by the outbreak of the second world war.

Meanwhile, the economy recovered along the established lines of export-oriented growth as did the world economy. Different to the pre-crisis economic cycle the capitalist nexus: sisal plantations and gold production contributed roughly 45 percent to Tanganyika's exports.[71]

The war affected Tanganyika in many ways. Changes in social dynamics and the colony's legal status[72] strengthened African nationalism which began to contest colonial rule.

The war economy led to economic transformation towards large-scale farming and extended peasant commoditisation. For reasons of scarce finances and capacities Tanganyika had to concentrate on high-valued agro-exports what foremostly favoured sisal whose export value more than doubled during the war years.

Also, the colony was forced into financial self-sufficiency which stimulated import substitution, on the one hand, and substantial wage cuts, on the other. While peasant commodity production benefited from the new constellation African wage labour was exposed to further material degradation.[73]

Both social strata conditioned nationalist politics in the post-war years. That wage labour, highly organised, rejected colonial capitalism for reasons of income and work conditions is evident. Their ranks were filled by ex-servicemen, conscripted and requisitioned labour who were laid off immediately after the war[74] what contributed to workers' militancy.

The aspiring peasantry criticised discriminatory pricing, marketing and taxation by the colonial state.[75]

---

[71] Cf. J.P. Moffett, J.F.R. Hill, *Tanganyika: A Review of Its Resources and Their Development*. Dar es Salaam, 1955, p.425, table 22.
[72] The Trusteeship status under the United Nations substituted for the League of Nations; the new forum improved the nationalist position which for the first time received international backing.
[73] Co-operative membership increased from 16,800 in 1933 to 33,400 for 1938 to 326,000 at the closing stage of colonialism; the number of independent cash farmers increased from 4,200 to 81,500 during the same period; cf. Stephens, Political Transformation of Tanganyika, p.38.
[74] After 1940 more than 73,000 Africans were conscripted for essential industries what equalled roughly one third of the pre-war work force; requisitioned labour for employment in public services amounted to 162,000; servicemen in auxiliary army functions totalled 311,000; cf. Moffett, Hill, Tanganyika, pp.269, 288.
[75] B.D. Bowles, 'The political economy of colonial Tanganyika 1939-1961', in M.H.Y. Kaniki (ed.), *Tanzania under Colonial Rule*. London, 1980, p.169.

The colonial power pursued its modernisation policy primarily for the economic requirements of metropolitan Britain and to a lesser extent for social containment.

Long-term development planning followed from the consolidation of Britain's position of world power. Metropolitan economic recovery was linked to colonial development that in the case of Tanganyika emphasised agro-export extension through crop diversification and large-scale, mechanised farming.[76] The formation of the Overseas Development Corporation and Overseas Food Corporation documented the new economic commitment towards colonial valorisation.[77] In the wake of this design colonial governments were instructed to two-years plans whose finances stemmed from colonial resources to be supplemented with metropolitan funds.[78]

In Tanganyika, export-orientation gathered momentum.[79] Sisal, the traditional export staple, was added by groundnuts and further crop diversification among the peasantry. The large-scale groundnut scheme originated from Britain's deficitary supplies with natural fats that had to be covered from own resources because of precarious balance of payments.[80]

However, the scheme failed because of inappropriate technology and mismanagement and became "nothing more than an over-large land-clearing exercise".[81]

The ensuing financial loss shifted the focus towards the accelerated modernisation of the co-operative societies that was partly funded through cuts of the welfare scheme.[82] Hereafter, modernisation policy generated those political cleavages which

---

[76] The Economist, July 13, 1946, p.46, defined this policy as continuation of the pre-war approach.
[77] Cf. The Economist, Nov.1, 1947, p.719; Nov.15, 1947, p.794.
[78] The Economist, March 25, 1947, p.364. For Tanganyika a ten-year development plan for the period 1947 to 1957 was drafted. It was based on capital spending in the range of £17.833 mio; Tanganyika, *Revised Development and Welfare Plan for Tanganyika 1950-1956*. Dar es Salaam, 1951, p.3. Approximately three quarters were to be financed from colonial sources with the rest funded by Britain; Tanganyika, *Statistical Abstract 1938-1952*. Dar es Salaam, 1954, p.40. The plan distinguished among development and welfare schemes. As regards development almost £7 million were to be spent on communications out of the total £8.621 million. Welfare schemes mainly consisted in town development which absorbed roughly £3 mio; The Economist, March 15, 1947, p.365. Eventually, one quarter of the funds came from the Colonial Development Fund; loan funds covered almost 50 percent; territorial sources contributed the missing amount; according to Moffett, Hill, Tanganyika, pp. 844f, economists with the colonial administration.
[79] Exports rose from £8.6 mio in 1945 to £26.5 million in 1950 and amounted to £58.9 million at independence; D.A. Low and Alison Smith (ed.), *History of East Africa*. Vol. III. Oxford, 1976. Statistical Appendix, p.588, app.III, table 7.
[80] A. Wood, *The Groundnut Affair*. London, 1950, p.344; The Economist, March 15, 1947, p.365.
[81] Sally H. Frankel, 'The Kongwa Experiment', *The Colonial Review*, 6, 8, 1950, p.239. The scheme's failure is documented by The Economist, March 5, 1949, p.405; March 19, 1949, p.505; May 14, 1949, p.880; Nov. 5, 1949, pp.989f, and Nov.4, 1950, p.683. For the political aspects see Kenneth O. Morgan, *Labour in Power 1945-1951*. Oxford, 1984, pp.201f, 231.
[82] Welfare schemes had absorbed 46 percent of capital investment; under the new conditions, this share contracted to 32 percent; The Economist, March 15, 1947, p.365; Moffett, Hill, Tanganyika, pp.844f.

eventually laid the ground for independence:[83] The support for peasant commercialisation introduced capitalistic elements into the countryside while the welfare cuts contributed to the already explosive urban situation. In a very short time, colonial rule antagonised the two most important social strata.

In colonial development planning co-operative societies acted as the economic vehicle of progress in peasant relations of production. They should meet various objectives that included the zeal of material improvement through economic means with the hope of rendering the traditional social values obsolete. Furtheron, the binding of economic ties between peasantry and colonial state aimed at political stability of colonial rule. Against this background, the extension of commercialised production would benefit merchant capital and the agro-processing industries in metropolitan Britain.[84]

The peasantry's march into the market accompanied the restructuring of traditional relations of production as the increase of the marketable share of the peasant production made the re-organisation of family/gender labour necessary; in addition, the extended monetisation eroded the subsistence backbone of peasant production apparently because of the comparative advantages of cash production. Finally, the co-operative societies followed market regulations in regards of decision-making and control so that social stratification was enhanced.

Short-term advantages notwithstanding, this model of rural modernisation must lack perspective and stability for two obvious reasons. First, modernisation implies social reconstruction what necessitates a committed government which must be accessible and open to adjustment. Second, modernisation implies the irreversible shift towards commercialisation what necessitates the state economic policy of protection.

---

[83] Modernisation covered the whole range of net world market integration, putting out in the case of the Urrambo tobacco growers, raw material supplies to British textile industries as in Sukumaland, food production of the Ismani and Iraqw capitalist farmers, and soil conservation schemes in the Usambaras and Ulugurus. These schemes co-existed with regions whose pattern of integration remained unaltered such as the Makonde, Ha, and Ngoni labour reserves for the sisal plantation economy and the Northern Rhodesian copper industries; cf. Iliffe, History of Modern Tanganyika, pp.463, 469f; Goran Hyden, *Beyond Ujamaa in Tanzania. Underdevelopment and an Uncaptured Peasantry*. London, 1980, pp.56f. This connection did not lead to proletarisation for the following reasons. Farms and plantations in Tanganyika as elsewhere in colonial Africa produced basic, interchangeable agro-products which competed with similar products. Therefore, cost cutting became pivotal. Persistent dependency on natural conditions forced farms and plantations into following the seed-harvest cycle. Both observations explain the policy of reduced overhead costs that translated into the employment of seasonal, migratory labour.

[84] On the level of planning, co-operatives accompanied the abolition of independent middlemen and their substitution by state marketing boards through which two objectives were met. First, the boards introduced new crop varieties and agro-techniques that promised higher returns for the state while, at the same time, binding the peasantry even closer to the state; cf. Andrew Coulson, *Tanzania. A political economy*. Oxford, 1982, pp.62f.

Both conditions did not exist in colonial Tanganyika where peasant modernisation was unprotectedly exposed to market forces and discrimination.[85]

The economic gains disappear once the economic cycle contracts. But, the new social relations based on commercialisation can no longer be maintained while the return to the old order is precluded. Peasant opposition, therefore, was apparent.[86] Exactly this constellation characterises the situation in Tanganyika in the mid-fifties.[87]

The crisis of modernisation collided with the crisis of the colonial system because the economic results, on the one hand, were too small while the social costs of modernisation had destroyed the former policy of co-option, on the other. In this situation, the rise of urban protest defeated the beleaguered colonial state.[88]

At the same time, international politics affected Tanganyika; the United Nations called for independence of its trusteeship territory[89] what Britain, eventually, had to accept.[90] The race for power buried politics other than mere nationalism that together with the colonial legacy in the economic arena formed the major obstacle against post-colonial development.[91]

---

[85] In successful regions such as Kilimanjaro, Sukumaland, Iringa and Iraqw transformation into rural capitalism was owed to the immediate producers who carried out plan and design against the colonial state. This confidence fostered their position in the political struggle for independence where they sided with the nationalist cause of *Tanganyika Kujitawala* (Tanganyika self-rule); cf. John C. de Wilde, *Experiences with Agricultural Development in Tropical Africa*. Vol. II. The Case Studies. Baltimore, 1967, p.444.

[86] Bowles, 'The political economy of colonial Tanganyika', pp.14f. Changes introduced from outside were regarded as interventionist that outline the basics of peasant resilience.

[87] The quest for monetisation forced the colonial state into extended market relations of regions which had previously resisted the cash nexus and had opted for wage labour instead in order to meet tax obligations. Precisely as the new cash nexus was delegated to merchant middlemen economic discrimination prevailed that blocked social advances; cf. Iliffe, History of Modern Tanganyika, p.466.

[88] Nationalism embarked from the urban centres but owed its rapid success to peasant pressure; cf. G.A. Maguire, *Toward 'Uhuru' in Tanzania. The Politics of Participation*. Cambridge, 1969, passim.

[89] The Tanganyika trusteeship was regularly debated and its affairs inspected by UN missions in a three-year interval. Indeed, the first mission recommended 'the establishment of a common voting role, a common citizenship, and a Tanganyika nationality'; Africa Digest May/June 1955, p.18. These recommendations shocked public opinion in East Africa in the words of Lord Twining, the British governor; Edward Twining, 'The last nine years in Tanganyika', *African Affairs*, 50, 201, 1959, p.17. Following the Chapter 12 of the UN Charter the mission insisted on the preparation for self-government and also urged that national representatives should become members of the Trusteeship Council; Margaret L. Bates, 'Social Engineering, Multi-racialism, and the Rise of TANU: the Trust Territory of Tanganyika 1945-1961', in D.A. Low and Alison Smith (ed.), *History of East Africa*. Vol. III. Oxford, 1976, pp.174f.

[90] Bates, 'Social Engineering, Multi-racialism, and the Rise of TANU', p.193.

[91] National independence appeared as the only possible alternative against colonial rule. This pattern persisted after independence when colonial rule was substituted for neo-colonial dependence. In consequence, social and economic problems were subsumed under nationalist priorities that prohibited a civil society for years to come; cf. M.H.Y. Kaniki (ed.), *Tanzania under Colonial Rule*. Oxford, 1980, p.365.

3. Railways in Tanganyika

Mechanisation of transport systems appeared as the most appropriate vehicle of capitalist valorisation in the age of early industrialisation.[92] The railway construction in Tanganyika, therefore, documents the embryonic state of colonial capitalism and the retarded state of development.[93]

Mechanised transport systems formed the backbone of the colonial economies, German and British;[94] similar to and almost identical with British rule German colonialism relied on railways as the vehicle of economic advance and valorisation.[95] According to the contemporary economist Jahn,[96] the cost per one freight ton amounted to 2,250 marks for caravans but to less than 130 marks for railways.[97]

---

[92] "The railway, with its allies the electric telegraph and the steamship, virtually annihilated distance and became at one bound the most potent physical influence on the development of the world in the nineteenth century"; Michael Robbins, *The Railway Age*. London, 1962, p.2.

[93] Cf. Rosa Luxemburg, *Die Akkumulation des Kapitals. Ein Beitrag zur ökonomischen Erklärung des Imperialismus*. Archiv sozialistischer Literatur 1. Frankfurt, 1966, p.335.

[94] Railway construction in colonial Africa differed from the rest of the colonial world for reasons of finance and economic stimulation. Railways were financed through guaranteed fixed-interest-bearing loans that had to be repaid irrespective of the economic cycle; regarding the second factor, colonial Africa entered into stagnation once "the first fine frenzy of pioneering was over". The railway infrastructure had not been followed by the expected proliferation of secondary development; Charles Wilson, 'The Economic Role And Mainsprings Of Imperialism', in Peter Duignan and L.H. Gann (ed.), *Colonialism in Africa 1870-1960*. Volume Four. The Economics of Colonialism. Cambridge, 1975, p.87.

[95] The official history of German railway construction is written by Deutsche Kolonial-Eisenbahn-Bau und Betriebsgesellschaft, *Von der Küste zum Kilimanjaro*. Berlin, n.d. The publication of the Kolonialpolitisches Aktionskomittee, *Die Eisenbahnen Afrikas. Grundlagen und Gesichtspunkte für eine koloniale Eisenbahnpolitik*. Berlin, 1907 defended the railway politics in the light of the financial scandal as did F. Balzer, *Die Kolonialbahnen mit besonderer Berücksichtigung Afrikas*. Berlin und Leipzig, 1916. Notably E. Zimmermann, *Die ostafrikanische Zentralbahn, der Tanganyikaverkehr und die ostafrikanischen Finanzen*. Berlin, 1911, and Walter Rathenau, 'Erwägungen über die Erschließung des Deutsch-Ost-afrikanischen Schutzgebietes'. (1907) in *Nachgelassene Schriften*. Band II. Berlin, 1928 were very sceptical of official policy. Under the impact of fascism, railways were discussed under geo-political auspices; see E. Randzio und K. Remy, *Kolonialbahnen. Die Koloniale Verkehrspolitik in Afrika*. Berlin, 1942. At a later date, H. Schroeter, *Die Eisenbahnen der ehemaligen deutschen Schutzgebiete*. Frankfurt, 1961, epitomises the railway technology and follows the uncritical path of African railway history.

[96] G.K. Jahn, 'Rückblick auf die Fortschritte unserer kolonialen Entwicklung', in *Jahrbuch über die deutschen Kolonien*, 1, 1908, p.65.

[97] Could porterage have solved the economic requirements even of the nascent colonial economy? Evidently not because of bulk cargoes from the plantation sector while the handling of import commodities was highly inefficient. Moreover, porterage-based transportation was labour- and time-intensive what caused delays in capital turnover and increasing overhead costs. Porterage was not compatible with the modern economy even under conditions of conscript labour. Mechanised transport, thus, became pivotal, and against the background of available technology this, automatically, implied railways.

I.

The Tanga Line, the first railway to be built in German East Africa, mirrors corruption, inefficiency, and mismanagement.[98] Immediately after the beginning of track laying the railway company, by that time a subsidiary of the Deutsche Ostafrika Gesellschaft, faced the first labour shortage. Thus, the completion of the first section from Tanga to Mushea, a distance of mere forty kilometres, took almost three years.

The next delay resulted from financial difficulties and the necessary new financial arrangements so that the work on the second section from Mushea to Korogwe commenced in July 1899. The original labour force numbered only 400 to 450 men, but by January 1900 it rose to 800 and six months later to 2,000 African workers.[99] The work was let out to numerous small contractors with the idea that competition would stipulate the progress of work. However, these contractors lacked adequate resources, capital and managerial, and were far too inexperienced for the project. That more than one quarter of the African workers at one time were either sick or unable to work outlines the combination of contractors' incompetence and their quest for rapid profits. Meanwhile, the German Consul-General at Zanzibar started confidential talks with British officials in Mombasa about Indian workers for Deutsch Ostafrika.[100]

Three years later, the Imperial Treasury signed a contract with the company of Lenz & Co., a German firm of railway contractors, for the construction of the next leg of the Tanga Line. Again, labour shortages persisted; the contracting company proposed the use of force which the Colonial Office in Berlin objected as did the colonial Labour Department. The Governor urged the company for adequate wages to be regarded as the most appropriate solution to the labour crisis. The Tanga-Line was completed in August 1904, and in the words of Hill, the chronicler of the East African railways: "It had taken twelve years to build 129 Kms whereas construction of the Uganda Railway started in the December of 1895 and the first locomotive ran to Kisumu, 572 miles from Mombasa, on December 20th, 1901."[101]

---

[98] J. Waldmann, *Usambara railway construction*. Oxford, 1956, gives the most accurate account. H. Wettich, *Die Entwicklung Usambaras unter Einfluß der ostafrikanischen Nordbahn*. Leipzig, 1911 extrapolates the economic potentials of the railway construction.
[99] On labour recruitment and conditions of employment see Reichskolonialamt, *Amtliche Jahresberichte. Die deutschen Schutzgebiete in Afrika und der Südsee 1909/10*. Berlin, 1910, p.55.
[100] For the following see Rainer Tetzlaff, *Koloniale Entwicklung und Ausbeutung. Wirtschafts- und Sozialgeschichte Deutsch-Ostafrikas 1885-1914*. Berlin, 1970, pp.82-6.
[101] M.F. Hill, *Permanent Way*. Vol II. The Story of the Tanganyika Railways. Nairobi, 1957, pp.72-3.

The striking contrast between the two railways reflects on the lack of competence and the early reluctance of the Imperial Government on colonial affairs.[102] The change of government and the following quest for *Weltmacht* after Bismarck's dismissal translated into the new colonial commitment. The new policy approach is evidenced by the construction of the Central Line, the famous *Mittellandbahn*, which connected the Swahili coast with Lake Tanganyika.[103]

Construction began in 1905 but faced immediate labour shortages due to the Maji Maji rebellion. Arrangements were prepared for the import of Chinese kuli labour but the solution came from sources nearer home. The Wanyamwezi, the porters of the 19th century caravan trade and thus conversant with wage labour, accepted the construction work. By the standards of the day, they were well paid and well fed, a new approach which reflected on the impact of the Maji Maji rebellion as is documented by the official report on "The Labour Problems Arising from the Opening Up of German East Africa by Means of a System of Public Transport". This report was commissioned immediately after the rebellion. Also, the labour situation owed much to Greek subcontractors who were responsible for the maintenance of the large labour force which, in peak periods, amounted to 20,000 men.

In less than nine years and more than sixteen months ahead of scheduled time, this railway line of c. 1,200 Kilometres reached Kigoma at Lake Tanganyika in early August 1914.

However, efficiency and productivity cannot be separated from the extremely high social costs. According to official reports (Amtliche Jahresbericht für 1911 by Reichskolonialamt) time wage was substituted for piece wage. Henceforth, the daily performance per worker amounted to a minimum 2.5 cubic metres of removed earth. In comparison, the construction of the Congo Line from Stanleyville to Lake Albert demanded a daily duty of 0.85 cubic metres.[104] And the Congo-Line was notorious for its poor work conditions. Topographical particularities notwithstanding, the Central Line must have been extremely exploitative what, indirectly, is admitted by the Co-

---

[102] Initially, the opening of the Tanga Line stimulated exports; according to Jahn, 'Rückblick auf die Fortschritte unserer kolonialen Entwicklung', p.66, exports through German customs stations amounted to less than 0.5 million marks but climbed to 3.75 million marks after the line opening.
[103] On the military importance of the new line see H.H. Graf von Schweritz, 'Bedarf Deutsch-Ostafrika jetzt einer Zentralbahn?', in *Koloniales Jahrbuch*, 9, 1897, pp.16-30.
[104] D. Kirchhoff, 'Die Eisenbahnen im östlichen Kongostaat', in *Zeitschrift für Kolonialpolitik, Kolonialrecht und Kolonialwirtschaft*, 9. 1907, p.270.

lonial Office which in the above-quoted report states that no worker voluntarily extends his six-months contract.

Enforced modernity implied the valorisation of the colonial economy and the subordination of its resources under the metropolitan core. This politico-economic pattern owed its existence to the railways; railway financing exposes the predominant role of the imperial state and the apparently long-term ambitions of metropolitan big industry headed by the leading banks.

The Tanga-Line mirrors the early concept of German colonialism, the amalgamation of over-ambitious, yet inexperienced settlers and the DOAG concession company which like the British chartered companies set out for a rapid plunder only to harvest disappointing results.[105] Less than seven years after the DOAG charter its subsidiary company, the Eisenbahngesellschaft für Ostafrika, went bankrupt in whose wake the Imperial Government cancelled the charter contract; acquired the railway and all its assets for 1.3 million marks and placed a first instalment of 250,000 marks for the extension work to the Korogwe railhead. One year later, the Reichstag approved a 2.3 million marks grant for the extension to be topped up by another one million as a final instalment. For reasons of domestic politics the grant to extend the railway beyond Korogwe was withheld by the Reichstag for another two years. Eventually, the Imperial Government and the colonial administration were not prepared for a state-owned railway in East Africa so that the Deutsche Eisenbahn Bau- und Betriebsgesellschaft was established as a wholly owned subsidiary of Lenz & Co., the contractor company. In return for the concession, the company paid an annual rent of 152,000 marks to the Imperial Treasury, to be fixed at some 250,000 marks by 1909 and to 760,000 once the railway achieved full-scale operation. This financial arrangement must be put into a social perspective for the following reasons.[106]

Even though the company balance sheets showed a regular surplus, it remained rather dubious under solid accountancy. The company never kept any reserve capital to be used for repair works and replacement of rolling stocks. Empirical evidence supports this assessment: in 1913 gross revenue amounted to 1,182,321 marks with running costs of c. 883,000 marks. The annual surplus, therefore, failed to cover the

---

[105] Cf. Tetzlaff, Koloniale Entwicklung und Ausbeutung, pp.82-3.
[106] Cf. Iliffe, Modern History of Tanganyika, pp.136-7, and C.W. Leverett, 'An Outline of the History of Railways in Tanganyika', in *Tanganyika Notes and Records*, 46, 1957, pp.108-116.

annual rent of 760,000 marks which, in turn, was significantly less than the interest charges of about one million marks per year - a financial constellation which necessitates further analysis not only with regard to the railway company but also to colonial policy.[107]

It seems that the company highly inflated the real value of its assets particularly as net revenues remained constantly below the annual rent transfers. This unreliable policy, most likely, has its origins in speculation - apparently, the long-term gains from railway-induced valorisation prevailed over solid business administration.

Railway finance also suggests the broader ambitions of the Imperial Government whose covered subsidies kept the railway company going. But, the underlying modalities portrayed a clear-cut infringement of the constitutional regulations. It, therefore, becomes evident that the Reich regarded the railways as the - literally - necessary vehicle for its quest of colonial development.

From here follow some observations: The company did not hesitate to manipulate its economic results; it was also prepared for an exploitative employment policy; and the colonising state was prepared for a similar approach propelled by the aforementioned policy objective or, in the words of Hill: "Of itself the Nordbahn (Tanga-Line) was never an economic proposition and the capital invested in it could only be justified by the economic development of the countryside which made it possible."[108]

The factual state of the Tanga railways is aptly summarised by Gillman, the railway engineer and Chief Engineer of the (British) Tanganyika Railways: Many rails were badly aligned; the African work force was not sufficiently skilled while the European trackmen would not give satisfactory service as they were allowed to own plantations along the line or to work for plantation owners as well as for the railway.[109]

In the last pre-war year, the Tanga railway traffic staff consisted of 400 African workmen, 46 African artisans, 42 Indian artisans, and 36 European officials while the construction staff was composed of more than 4,000 African workers and 50 European supervisors.[110]

As regards the Central Line, Imperial Government participation was even more pronounced. After a series of lengthy preliminary investigations which started in the

---

[107] Cf. Tetzlaff, Koloniale Entwicklung und Ausbeutung, pp.84-5.
[108] Hill, Permanent Way. Vol II, p.78.
[109] C. Gillman, 'A Short History of the Tanganyika Railways', in *Tanganyika Notes and Records*, 13, 1942, pp.14-55.
[110] Reichskolonialamt, *Amtlicher Jahresbericht 1911/2*. Berlin, 1912, p.13.

mid-90s the colonial council (Kolonialrat) eventually resolved in October 1899 that the Central Line should be built. Its advocating on a railway policy conscious of its aim to counter the competition of neighbouring colonies not only matched the Imperial Government's over-all policy ambitions but also took the extension of the German sphere of influence in Central Africa into account.[111]

Notably, Deutsche Bank held prospecting concessions in Katanga and interests in Congo shipping what explains the bank's commitment in Tanganyika railway construction.[112]

A syndicate headed by Deutsche Bank prepared the foundation of the Ostafrika Eisenbanhngesellschaft with an initial capital of 21 million marks. The Imperial Government granted the company the right of a corporation and a concession to build and run a metre-gauge railway from Dar es Salaam to Morogoro and guaranteed the payment of a 3 per cent interest on company capital. The Eisenbahngesellschaft gave contract to Ph. Holzmann AG, the constructor of the Baghdad Bahn. Many of the company staff and several subcontractors who had worked in the Middle East transferred to Tanganyika. Four years later, the Dar-Morogoro section was completed and the Reichstag approved the railway extension from the Morogoro railhead to Lake Tanganyika. The Eisenbahngesellschaft retained its concessions and received a colonial administration loan of 80 million marks, the estimated cost of extension work. The Reich guaranteed a 4 per cent interest on the loan. For collateral security, the Dar-Morogoro section was mortgaged to the colonial administration. Once each section on the extension was completed it was also mortgaged, and 95 per cent of the Eisenbahn-gesellschaft's initial share capital was purchased by the colonial administration - the Central Line turned into a state railway operated by the Eisenbahngesellschaft as a public utility company.[113]

In terms of efficiency, the Central Line was great success. But precisely because of the vested interests of the investing companies and the Reich the pressure must have been enormous and must also have affected the organisation of the work force of

---

[111] On the strategic designs in the wake of the 1906' reforms see *inter alia* R.V.Pierand, 'The Dernberg Reform Policy and German East Africa', in *Tanzania Notes and Records*, 67, 1967, pp.31-8.
[112] Cf. George W.F. Hallgarten, *Imperialismus vor 1914. Die soziologischen Grundlagen der Außenpolitik europäischer Großmächte vor dem ersten Weltkrieg*. Zweiter Band. München, 1963, pp.228, 424.
[113] *Jahrbuch über die deutschen Kolonien*, 1, 1908, p.65; 2, 1909, pp.72, 283; 3, 1910, pp.218, 258; 5, 1912, p.67.

16,000 construction workers and c. 3,600 traffic staff, and, obviously, the labour relations at construction site.[114]

In economic terms, German Ostafrika showed disappointing results with exports amounting to 31 mio. Marks by 1912 that equalled less than 60 percent of the entire export trade of all German colonies. But, imports rose to almost 50 mio. Marks in the same year. Even though this imbalance is attributed to the railway building material and the rolling stocks it outlines the very fragile economic foundations of German colonialism.

The plantation economy still looked for a new centre of gravity once the rubber boom had resulted in the 1911 collapse after which date colonial rubber failed to attract customers even in metropolitan Germany.

Sisal, the new alternative, was promising but remained insignificant in general economic terms. In spite of their commitment the settlers lacked the capital funds for large-scale farming with their survival mainly owed to official support and subsidies such as conscript labour and preferential tariffs and tax exemption.[115]

Even worse, and the major reason for failure, German big industry barely invested in the colonies which absorbed less than 4 per cent of total German foreign investment.[116]

The economic calamities defined the colony's status of backwater.[117]

German colonialism in Africa originated from Bismarck's sophisticated and masterly orchestrated diplomacy in a much wider game for German world power. It, at same time, contributed to chauvinist currents connected with colonialism which in the post-Bismarck period gave support to the political maze. It now appeared that the African colonies could be exploited for geo-political ambitions - the *Mittelafrika-Konzept* through which British hegemony should be challenged.[118] In addition, the access to

---

[114] Reichskolonialamt, *Amtlicher Jahresbericht 1913*. Berlin 1913, tab.B.I.2.
[115] In 1912, the area under cultivation was less than 81,000 ha of which rubber accounted for 32,000 ha. During this year, more than 50,000 ha. were transferred and/or auctioned; according to Reichskolonialamt, Amtlicher Jahresbericht 1913, B II.1, pp.66-84.
[116] According to Herbert Feis, *Europe the World's Banker*. New Haven, 1930, pp.60-78. His computations show a total investment stock in the colonies of c. 600 mio. Marks in 1914; German direct investment accounted for approximately 85 percent.
[117] For a detailed account see L.H. Gann, 'Economic Development in Germany's African Empire, 1884-1914', in Peter Duignan and L.H. Gann (ed.), Colonialism in Africa 1870-1960, pp.213-53.
[118] Geo-politics emerged during the debate in the mid-thirties on Germany's renewed request for the former colonies. F.S. Joelson, *Germany's claims to Colonies*. London, 1939, detects the planning by German colonial officials of a 'Mittelafrika', the colonial empire that would stretch from the Upper Guinee coast, the Congo to northern Moçambique. The conquest would be launched from Tanganyika, and therefore railways were needed.

Katangese copper was another reason for railway construction in Tanganyika. The Annual Reports of the Tanganyika Railways (after 1920) frequently refer to these aspects when discussing low capacity utilisation and the ensuing financial deficits of the central railway line. Although historical studies on German East Africa neglect this factor British authorities reasoned on the military design precisely as the Central Line was built in record time and with unrestricted financial resources.

Apart from the settler pockets and the plantations along the coastal belt and its immediate hinterland the colony remained the realm of peasant producers. However, even the limited capitalist penetration inflicted social change on the African societies. The formerly most advanced peasant societies were driven into labour exporting areas because of land alienation and the subsequent denial of market access. It seems, therefore, that the railway system at the extended scale exceeded the economic potentials what, in turn, explains the persistent financial deficits.

To summarise, railway construction in German East Africa did not facilitate capitalistic valorisation as it followed geo-political objectives and economic requirements of the settlers, a more or less redundant economic element. In other words, German colonialism was hybrid. Hybridity refers to the grand ambitions, on the one hand and the meagre operational results, on the other.

II.

Tanganyika under the British Mandate was the second beginning due to impact, effect, and outcome of the war in East Africa, a secondary theatre of the world war but one of primordinary significance for the East African peoples. The *Kleinkrieg* devastated the country, its human and economic resources. Reconstruction after the armistice faced a destroyed modern infrastructure while the African population, faminised by the guerrilla warfare, suffered from diseases. On top of that, the British mandatory power had to re-organise the ownership relations at the plantations and the settler farms.

In the words of a memorandum tabled for the German Imperial Cabinet in July 1918 (sic!): "The policy [...] both of Australia and India might be very strongly influenced by pressure from German *Mittel-Afrika*, and British policy too, since England has a strong interest in unimpeded commercial intercourse with India and Australia, as India and Australia have in unimpeded intercourse with England. If we have a position of strength in *Mittel-Afrika*, then we can compel India and Australia to respect our wishes in the South Seas and in Eastern Asia"; (pp.122-3).

Britain succeeded German colonialism in the administration of the Tanganyika territory. The Mandate covenant regulated the ownership of former German possessions; the two railway lines accounted among the most valuable assets which could play a strategic role in the colony's future valorisation.

However, the take-over portrayed a series of difficulties and obstacles what in the case of the railways related to their devastated state.[119] The receding German armies had destroyed the major bridges and tracks[120] in order to deny the British logistical assets in what was a very bizarre military campaign. The British armies relied on the railways for transport but lacked adequate spare parts. Thus, at armistice the railways were in a deplorable state and substantial repair work for this reason imperative.[121]

But above all, the legal and financial position of the railways awaited settlement.[122] In a wider perspective the railways' role in the future economic policy had to be assessed and how a synchronised approach could be achieved. What appeared as being of vital interest for Tanganyika presented itself in a different light for Britain. This hiatus helps to understand why necessary reconstruction work as well as policy formulation took some years before realisation.

The official policy approach towards Tanganyika might be summarised as follows. Different to German colonialism Britain in Tanganyika embarked on a neatly identified objective that can be defined as the peasantisation of the economy. Precisely because of Britain's financial constraints the support for peasant producers formed the most adequate policy of valorisation. This support substantiated in extended social engineering schemes such as the early co-operative societies movement. It also contributed to the social and political consciousness of the colonised Africans what was widely favoured by the new generation of colonial administrators. Eventual-

---

[119] For the railway take-over see N. Bentwich, *The Mandates System*. London, 1930, pp.180-4.
[120] All ten of the Tanga Railway's major bridges had been severely damaged by the Germans, and 23 minor bridges were blown up; most of the water tanks and pumps were destroyed as were 30 miles of track which were picked up and thrown into the bush, and 60 sets of points and crossings were damaged. On the Central Line most of the damage was between Dar es Salaam and Dodoma. 92 major bridges and 14 minor bridges were either blown up or severely damaged as were more than 100 sites of points and crossings, and most of the watering stations were damaged; cf. The Secretary of State for the Colonies, *Report of the Railway System of Tanganyika Territory by Brigadier-General F.D. Hammond*. London, 1930, p.8.
[121] According to Tanganyika Territory, *Report on Tanganyika Territory for 1920*. Dar es Salaam, 1920, p.52, the official costs were given as follows. Damage done to the Tanga Line: RS 2,195,000 (c.£146,000); for the Central Line: RS 2,946,581 (c.£196,000).
[122] The financial aspects are discussed by G.L. Beer, *African Questions at the Paris Peace Conference with papers on Egypt, Mesopotamia, and the colonial settlement*. London, 1923, pp.158ff., and G.L. Steer, *Judgment on German Africa*. London, 1939, pp.162ff.

ly, it was hoped that hereby the colony's financial autonomy could be achieved. This approach translated into the pivotal role of the railways, to be recognised as artery and backbone on whose performance the success of peasantisation came to rest.

With regard to the railways the early years of British rule fall under three levels: (i) the pragmatic work of physical recovery; (ii) the formulation of a railway policy in congruence with overall colonial policy, and (iii) the settlement of finances which accompanied the former.

On both the Tanga and the Central Line permanent repairs were started in 1919.[123] Almost three years later the repair work was accomplished. Apart from the track it was also necessary to undertake a considerable repair work for station buildings and staff quarters. For lack of funds more than the most urgent repairs could not be performed. Staff housing faced another obstacle as the Germans only provided quarters for the European staff of the railways while many of the Asian and all of the African staff had to look for accommodation for themselves.[124]

The Tanganyika Railways inherited from the Germans 20 goods engines; 22 tank engines; seven Mallet engines, and six shunting tank engines. To these engines deployed on the Central Line were added seven engines which operated the Tanga railways. It was estimated that the German goods engines would last for another twelve years, the tank engines for ten years, and that new engines would not be required until and unless a substantial increase in traffic occurred.[125] In spite of heavy spending on reconditioning the German engines they had to be scrapped as soon as fresh funds were available to buy new British engines.[126]

These efforts notwithstanding, the economic performance of the Tanganyika Railways remained poor notably due to the Central Line. Having been built for mainly military objectives[127] the civic conversion proved to be difficult particularly as only the first 280 kilometres of the coastal zone show good traffic prospects while the remaining 960 kilometres pass through undeveloped country with the exception of the

---

[123] For a detailed account see the following chapter.
[124] According to Tanganyika Territory, *Report on Tanganyika Territory for 1929*. Dar es Salaam 1929, p.31, the railways employed 146 Europeans, 645 Asians, and 6,334 Africans, including labourers.
[125] By the end of 1921 one passenger train and one goods train ran once a week in each direction between Dar es Salaam and Kigoma, and a mixed train ran once a week in each direction between Dar es Salaam and Tabora.
[126] To these added the capacity constraints of the erecting shops at Dar es Salaam, Tabora, and Tanga. The number of engines that could be handled at the same time was five in the Tabora shops, two in Dar es Salaam, and three in the Tanga shops. The engine pits suffered from the use of overhead cranes to lift the engines what resulted in delays and slow work progress.
[127] As was openly admitted by the German officials, see *inter alia* Koloniales Jahrbuch, 9,1897, pp.16-30.

Usoki salt works; in short, less than one third of the Central Line can be considered of generating a paying traffic.

Heavy expenditures for reconstruction and continuing deficits in the railways' operations[128] required an in-depth analysis for future solutions. This analysis should also help to adjust the railway policy to colonial development.

The first Hammond-Report[129] was to investigate the possibility of improvement in all departments of the railway systems of Kenya, Uganda and Tanganyika. The report's findings, published in November 1921, outlined that i) 'revenue falls far short of what is required to meet actual working expenses exclusive of renewals or loan charges'; ii) the accumulated heavy loss results from the 'very poor traffic which the two railways are carrying, while the expenses of maintaining a system of 1,747 kilometres long are bound to remain high, however reduced the service may be'.[130]

As for the Central Line, the report argued that financial improvement was seen to depend on the economic development of the Lake Tanganyika basin and the trade with the Congo. This assessment fell in line with the Belgian government's decision to invest £20 million in the Congolese economic infrastructure.

Regarding skilled labour the report recommended the improvement of African skilled workers. The entire skilled work force in the Dar es Salaam moulding shops; the carriage fitting; the carpentry work at Tanga, and a good proportion of the engine-driving were performed by Africans. At the same time, the Tanganyika Railways faced difficulties in recruiting skilled labour and artisans in India for reasons of poor payment, housing and climate.

Against this background the report's further recommendations for railway extension are contradictory for mere financial reasons. The report clearly outlined that the railways' economic performance was intimately correlated to the general development of the Mandate territory in the absence of an efficient export-oriented industry. The lack of a strong private sector explains that the future development of Tanganyika depended on financial resources generated by the British state. This situation bore

---

[128] For the first three years under British civil administration the railways accumulated losses of nearly £175,000 in 1920, of almost £189,000 in 1921 and over £191,000 in 1922. It must be added that these losses did not consider neither interest payments nor depreciation.
[129] The Secretary of State for the Colonies, *Report on the Railway Systems of Kenya, Uganda and Tanganyika by Lieut.-Colonel F.D. Hammond*. London, 1921.
[130] It must be added that the colonial economy entered its second consecutive year of crisis with exports decreasing by 42 per cent in value terms and imports fell by 17.8 per cent; cf. Tanganyika Territory, *Trade Report for 1921*. Dar es Salaam, 1921.

new conflicts as the funds for consolidated railway finances lacked the overall economic development what, in turn, prohibited the railways' sound financial performance. Different to successful economic take-off strategies, as was the case in the industrialised societies, the Tanganyika Railways had to fail as the 'economic pull factor' in the colonial set-up.

The Treaty of Versailles settled the Mandatory status of Tanganyika which, consequently, included the ownership of the railways. Whereas the Tanga Line and the harbour works at Tanga had been property of the German Government the ownership of the Central Line was more complex because this line had been the property of a private company. Following a complicated case at the Dar es Salaam High Court the Government of Tanganyika acquired for £33,994 assets whose capital value was assessed as £4,895,000 as at April 1st, 1919;[131] the Railway Administration had to pay interest on only £33,994 of the original German capital.

An apparently favourable deal the British government had to cover the operational deficits of the railways in addition to the take-over costs.

Until 1922 the accumulated loss amounted to £1,393,137; in spite of cost management the next two years showed deficits at a lower level of £1,169,256. These losses were covered by free Imperial grants amounting to £408,169 in 1921 and 1922 plus repayable loans from the Imperial Exchequer over £2,385,891. In sum, the Tanganyika Railways received £ 231,667 in net fresh capital from the British government.

For capital expenditure related to efficiency improvement of operations the British state gave a loan of £250,000. This investment helped to improve the operational performance to what added the general economic recovery so that by 1926 an operating profit of £3,261 was made. By that time, capital expenditure amounted to £610,107 on the Central Line and to £184,905 on the Tanga Line. The Deficiency Account stood at £786,498. The Imperial Treasury had given free grants of £478,158. The Tanganyika Railways had raised repayable loans of £1,342,534.[132]

---

[131] The High Court came to the conclusion that the market value of the Central Line amounted to £600,000 plus interest on the privately owned share to the amount of £14,000. The interest of the German Government in the railway was calculated at £580,006 which led to the net amount of £33,994 to be paid to the Custodian of Enemy Property in respect of the Central Line; cf. W. Morris-Hale, 'British Administration in Tanganyika from 1920 to 1945 with special reference to the Preparation of Africans for Administration Positions'. Thèse, University of Geneva, 1969, ch.1.
[132] Loans and grants amounted to £1,820,692 of which £1,019,490 was allocated to capital expenditure; cf. Colonial Office, *Report by His Britannic Majesty's Government to the Council of the League of Nations on the Administration of Tanganyika Territory for the Year 1927*. London, 1927, p.17,43.

The factors which caused the poor performance have to be looked after i) the protracted recovery of the plantation economy, the territory's main exporter; ii) the poor condition of the railways' rolling stock and locomotives which rendered operating costs extremely high in relation to the volume of traffic; and iii) the unbalanced traffic as the coast-bound traffic exceeded the up-country traffic.[133]

In order to achieve balanced finances colonial government and the Railway Administration decided i) to increase traffic by building branch lines into potentially productive areas; ii) to further reduce working costs;[134] iii) to equip the railways with efficient locomotives[135] and rolling stock; and iv) to relay some sections for heavier traffic.[136]

These measures combined professional management with the risk taking optimism as regards Tanganyika's economic prospects; to this added the reliance on copper exports from the Belgian Congo.[137] Working cost reductions were imperative against the background of heavy deficits which showed only slow improvements. The construction of branch lines into undeveloped, yet potentially rich areas contradicted any cautious approach but was justified from a long-term development perspective.[138]

The extension of the railway system mirrored various interests which ranged from the settlers' request for infrastructure development to strategic concerns about the link with the Southern African railway system.

---

[133] This imbalance is explained by the geographical particularity: Dar es Salaam, the colony's capital city and centre of industry and commerce, is located at the coast; the hinterland traffic, therefore, was limited.
[134] Cost reduction also extends to fuelling. Wood was the only fuel used on the colony's two railways. The timber, once conveniently close to the lines, had been cut down so that the cost of supply increased due to longer distances. Therefore, coal from South Africa gradually substituted wire food. By 1930, coal was used by all engines on the Tanga Line and on the Central Line between Dar es Salaam and Dodoma. Around Tabora fire wood was still obtainable at lower costs, and it continued to be used as fuel. The average cost per ton of coal was c. Shs.32 in 1929 while the average cost of wood fuel was Shs.9/40 per 100 cu.ft. on the Central Line. The consumption of coal per engine kilometre averaged 29.77 lb. and 3.37 cu.ft. for wood fuel, respectively. Although for the moment coal fuelling was more expansive than wood the running costs would decline with the introduction of new locomotives; see Tanganyika Railways, Annual Report, 1930, p.12.
[135] In 1923, six new tender engines were imported from Britain for service on the Central Line; three years later, eleven new locomotives were imported from Britain in addition to nine smaller engines bought between 1927 and 1929.
[136] By 1926 the line from Dar es Salaam to Morogoro had been re-laid with new 55-lb. British standard track. In 1929 and 1930 a considerable length of the Tanga Line was re-laid. The outbreak of the global economic crisis brought further relay works to a halt; but the remaining light German track was strengthened by the insertion of two additional sleepers in each length of rail.
[137] The position of the Congolese copper mines in the highly competed market remained fragile for cost reasons because of the low grade ores processed and the high transport costs from Katanga to the East African coast. As long the market continued to grow these structural disadvantages were not relevant; however, under recession the high-cost Congolese mines were the first to suffer.
[138] For the fiscal year 1922/23 the Tanganyika Railways covered a total of 740,316 miles of which almost 200,000 or c.27 per cent were non-revenue earning. This highly unprofitable structure helps to understand the urgent quest for traffic increase through new branch lines; see Tanganyika Railways, Annual Report, 1923, pp.60ff.

Extension mainly referred to the Central Line where the Germans had started the branch line from Tabora through Kahama to Mwanza at Lake Victoria, one of the agriculturally most developed regions in Tanganyika.[139] The other projects, however, remained highly controversial.

The East African Commission of 1925, reporting to the Secretary of State for the Colonies,[140] unequivocally identified the new railway construction as the most important factor for further economic development. Consequently, its recommendations focused on i) the extension of the Tabora-Mwanza line to Shinyanga which would need another 140 miles of new track; ii) the extension of the Tanga Line from Moshi to Arusha; iii) the construction of the Lake Nyasa line from Ngerengere - at Km 145 of the Central Line - through the Kilombero Valley to Manda on Lake Nyasa; iv) the construction of a line from Moshi to Dodoma which would connect the colony's two railway systems; v) the re-opening of the Voi line connecting the Tanganyika Railways with the Uganda Railway.

The commission, thus, combined feasible solutions with visionary projects. Indeed, the Mwanza line was completed in April 1928 for the additional cost of £631,000 or £3,470 per kilometre. Also, the extension from Moshi to Arusha covered 86 kilometres. The construction work started in 1927 and was completed more than two years later.[141] The line consumed £316,000 or approximately £3,700 per kilometre.[142]

With regard to the Lake Nyasa line various reconnaissance and pre-feasibility studies were done after 1925. In 1929, the Railway Administration submitted a comprehensive report which underlined the enormous costs and technical difficulties. It stated that "a line from Dodoma to Fife could only be regarded, technically and economically, as impossible proposition which could in no circumstances be recommended".[143]

---

[139] The first 120 kilometres built by the Germans with all the culverts and almost all of the bridges complete were in a good state in spite of ten years of neglect. The light track lifted from the Central Line between Dar es Salaam and Morogoro was used for the 160 kilometres of the Mwanza line. Therefore, the cost of the line from Mwanza to Shinyanga amounted to only £262,577 or c. £1,335 per kilometre.
[140] The Secretary of State for the Colonies, *Report of the East African Commission*. Cmd 2387. London, 1925.
[141] The main difficulty which explains the slow progress of work was the bridging of several deep gorges along the skirts ' Mount Kilimanjaro and Mount Meru.
[142] This line was an economic failure. Having been built under the assumption to facilitate the settler farms' access to the railway as the cheapest means of transport the farmers continued to carry their products to nearby Moshi by road. Also, the re-opening of the Voi line which connects Moshi with the Uganda Railway contributed to the economic difficulties; its was estimated that the Uganda Railway takes about 75 per cent of the outward traffic from Moshi while the Tanganyika Railways covered approximately 70 per cent of all traffic going into Moshi; see Tanganyika Railways, Annual Report, 1925, p.26.
[143] 'Report on Preliminary Surveys to open up the South-West of Tanganyika', by C. Gillman, Chief Engineer, London 1929.

These factors notwithstanding, the settlers strongly urged for the construction of that line and submitted their proposals under the Imperial Colonial Development Act.[144] The controversial issue should be settled by another report commissioned by the Secretary of State. This task, again, was performed by Brigadier-General Hammond.[145]

His findings consisted in recommending the Kilosa-Fife route which should pass through Ifakara and Mpanga. He rejected the Dodoma-Iringa line for the lack of economic feasibility. Obviously, this recommendation did not suit the settlers.

Again, the colonial government intended to solve the controversial issue through another report. The new commission headed by Sir Sidney Henn recommended i) the immediate construction of a railway from Kilosa to Ifakara; ii) the construction of a railway from Dodoma to Ubena bound to the conditionality of twenty-year interest free capital support by the British government; and iii) the construction of a line from Kilosa to the vicinities of Korogowe.[146]

This time, the colonial government accepted the findings[147] and proceeded with the financial and technical modalities. The outbreak of the global economic crisis, however, stopped the plans that should be realised more than forty years later by the construction of the TaZaRa railway built with Chinese aid.[148]

The colony's economic profile was shaped by agrarian raw material exports which entered into a boom period in the second half of the twenties. The Tanganyika Railways profited accordingly: The finances improved and the operations became profitable. The operating profit increased from £17,650 in 1926/7 to £241,381 for the fiscal year 1930. Almost forty per cent of the Central Line's revenues, equal to thirty per cent of the Tanganyika Railways, originated from the Congolese copper exports for the attraction of which the colonial government granted low tariffs in combination with the exemption from import duties.[149] This dependence turned into an economic

---

[144] The Southern Highlands were regarded by the Kenyan settler community as the most promising alternative. Many farms in the Kenyan highlands had run into economic difficulties and faced ruin due to the lack of further state support.
[145] The Secretary of State for the Colonies, Report of the Railway System of Tanganyika Territory by Brigadier-General F.D. Hammond, ch.15: Future Policy and Development.
[146] Tanganyika Territory, *Report of the Tanganyika Railway Commission*. London, 1930, pp.5-9.
[147] Sir Donald Cameron, Colonial Governor of Tanganyika, explained his position in a dispatch report to the settler community what brought the controversy to an end; see Hill, Permanent Way. Vol.II, p.214.
[148] See Martin Bailey, *Freedom Railway. China and the Tanzania-Zambia Link*. London, 1976, pp.113-6, 154-6.
[149] According to the second Hammond Report, p.48.

disaster when the Congolese traffic came to a halt in the wake of the global economic Depression.[150]

Nevertheless, loan charges bit into the profits[151] and caused the railways' precarious financial basis particularly when the impending renewals for the next three years were taken into consideration. According to the second Hammond Report approximately £1,270,000 had to be invested for this purpose.

The railways, therefore, were badly equipped in capital terms to withstand the economic crisis after 1930. The colony's exports which exceeded £4 million in 1928 shrank to c.£1,9 million in 1931. Simultaneously, the colonial government revenues fell from £1,992,675 in 1930 to £1,552,368 one year later. The crisis, of course, affected the railways. The Congolese copper exports came to a complete stop what equalled, as has been shown, the loss of more than one third of the railways revenues.

Secondly, the harvests of 1930 and 1931 were very poor what translated into a further reduction of traffic. Thirdly, to make matters even worse, these years coincided with the large increase of interest charges as resulted from the loan arrangements of the mid-twenties. The Railway Administration acted accordingly. Its cost management consisted in the following measures:

- staff reduction of 3,064 which mainly affected the African work force of which more than 2,500, almost one quarter of the total, were laid off;[152]
- the Workshops and Stores Deport at Tabora were closed down;
- wages were heavily reduced;
- workshops staff were put on short time combined to wage cuts;
- artisans were put on daily pay rates;
- cuts in allowances.

This cost saving exercise reduced working expenditures by c.£245,000 or approximately one third of total expenditures. In 1932, revenues fell from £900,708 to £557,792 while expenditures were down to £514,600. In spite of the successful ad-

---

[150] While in 1930 the Tanganyika Railways had handled c. 34,000 tons of Congolese copper, the tonnage declined to c. 7,000 tons one year later and came to a complete stop in 1932; see Tanganyika Railways, Annual Report, 1932.
[151] Between 1926 and 1930 the Railways produced an accumulated gross profit of £830,092 from which loan charges of £638,048 were deducted. The net profits of £192,044 covered the liability against the colonial administration.
[152] The reductions were as follows: European Staff: 106; Asian Staff: 451; African Staff: 2,507.

justment the operating surplus of c.£43,000 did neither cover the provisions for renewals nor loan charges of £252,072.

Due to the colony's exposed position of a raw material exporting economy recovery from the world economic crisis was slow; the precarious finances for the colonial government and the railways persisted throughout the thirties.

Even though the colonial economy showed signs of recovery after 1934, if the export performance is taken as the yardstick of measurement, the railways suffered from low revenues. It was calculated that the break-even point in revenue terms was at £1 million[153] which the railways failed to achieve during the period under discussion.[154] On the other hand, the cost reduction management as having been installed at the outbreak of the crisis, was successful. At first glance, the railways were profitable again since 1935; but this success was owed to the deliberate neglect of a renewal fund. Thus, the railways' short-term profitability was bought for the erosion of substance: track maintenance, rolling stock and locomotive renewal. It could be expected that in the near future the running costs would rise with substantial borrowing for necessary investments impending. In other word, a serious financial crisis was programmed.[155]

Revenues rose to £662,296 in 1936 while expenditure was only £350,893; interest charges amounted to £322,435. One year later, revenues rose to £780,565 with expenditure of £384,913. Due to unfavourable climatic conditions the railways' revenues fell to £662,556 what resulted into a loss of £20,780 after interest charges. Also the next year showed disappointing results with revenue amounting to only £712,642 while expenditures stood at £426,947. After interest charges the net loss came to £25,890.

In comparison with other African railways the Tanganyika system portrayed an extremely low goods traffic density of 32,900 ton-miles which contrasted sharply with

---

[153] According to official calculations; see Tanganyika Railways, Annual Report, 1932; Report of the General Manager.
[154] The loss of the Congolese traffic could not be compensated; therefore, the post-crisis performance showed efforts for the improvement of the Tanganyika traffic.
[155] To this adds the financial losses as were inflicted by the Kenya and Uganda Railways: contrary to the agreements, the later reduced the tariffs what led to an even greater diversion of traffic away from the Tanganyika Railways. This affected the export trade from the Lake Victoria region which used the K.U.R. system. The settlement of 1937 provided for equal rates and the equal disbursement of profits between the two railways. In reality, however, the sublime diversion of profits persisted as the K.U.R. paid a fraction of the costs for the transit traffic through Tanganyika so that it accumulated a net profit of £93,000 by 1939. If all the traffic, in the words of the Tanganyika Railways' General Manager, had been moved by the Tanganyika route, the net revenue of these services would, broadly, have been increased by a like amount.[...] In effect, the taxpayers of Tanganyika (at present the poorest of the East African territories) are being asked to pay this amount to the railway users of Kenya and Uganda. It should be noted, too, that this arrangement results in the Kenya and Uganda Railways users obtaining a lower-rate level than they would otherwise enjoy"; Tanganyika Railways, Annual Report, 1939.

265,000 ton-miles for the K.U.R. and approximately 500,000 ton-miles for the South African Railways.

It was clear that the Tanganyika Railways needed a considerably greater volume of traffic for a solid financial status. The traffic increase depended on the colony's economic development. The achievement of the financial objective resulted from the outbreak of the world war and the new economic challenges even for the remote Tanganyika Mandate Territory.[156]

During the war years goods traffic increased from 236,512 tons to 357,359 what resulted in the revenue increase from £469,228 to £638,536; also, passenger traffic rose from 511,869 issued tickets to 1,524,087 in 1945. The related revenue augmented from £93,478 to £345,650. Thus, the railways doubled the break-even point of £1 million.

The allied war machinery in the Middle East needed Tanganyika raw materials, timber, sisal, flour, and meal in particular. The railways carried 7,500 tons of timber in 1939 and 30,000 tons in 1945. The transport of flour and meal increased from 7,644 tons to 20,428 during the same period.[157]

As regards the passenger traffic the increase was mainly owed to the movements of troops and refugees.

With the full utilisation of the Territory's manpower and physical resources from 1942 the traffic increased phenomenally from 36,841,000 passenger miles in 1940 to 136,368,000 by the end of the war.[158]

Due to these factors, the railways' financial position improved dramatically. In 1941, revenue increased to £841,616 while expenditure stood at £313,137. The ensuing net gain of £96,551 was the largest since 1927. One year later, revenue climbed considerably to £1,115,927 whereas expenditure came to £504,642; the net profit amounted to £296,009. The railways' profits for the remaining war years were £267,122 in 1943; £276,332 in 1944, and £225,441 in 1945.

---

[156] For the Tanganyika war economy see N.J. Westcott, 'The Impact of the Second World War on Tanganyika, 1939-1949', Ph.D.thesis, Cambridge University, 1982, pp.56-80, 107-66.
[157] Traffic grew steadily from the depression; the sharp recession of 1938/39 was followed by a steady growth as the Territory expanded its production in spite of light and poorly distributed rains. Between 1939 and 1945 the ton mileage increased from 45,238,000 to   81,441,000; cf. Tanganyika Railways, Annual Report, 1946, pp.1-3.
[158] Tanganyika Railways, Annual Report, 1946, p.1

These gains enabled the Railway Administration to reduce the liability to the colonial government to less than £300,000 in 1941 and to c.£84,000 one year later. At last, the much needed Renewal Fund was established. The initial capital inflow of £100,000 in 1942 was followed by allocations of £220,000 in 1943; £237,150 in 1944, and £193,900 in 1945.

The solid finances did not blind the authorities to the exceptional circumstances to which this situation was owed. The major post-war challenge was identified in the competition by road traffic which according to the report of the railways' Chief Engineer, J.R. Farquharson, operated at much lower costs estimated for the usual three ton truck at 70 cents per vehicle-mile.

After the war, the Labour government in London embarked on its new concept of state-centred planning.[159] For Tanganyika a ten-year development and welfare plan was designed in accordance with the new concept. From the estimated plan costs of £19,186,000 over £3,5 million was reserved for road construction and improvement what clearly mirrored the change of policy priorities from the railways to the road system. In spite of this, the Tanganyika Railways pursued its programme of modernisation to which is was stimulated by the demands from the East African Groundnuts Scheme. The Scheme intended the large-scale valorisation of undeveloped farm land in Southern Tanganyika for the production of groundnuts for the British food processing industry. This grandiose scheme whose costs exceeded £100 million required goods handling and traffic. In 1947 and 1948, the scheme's peak years, the railways carried more than 34,000 tons and 58,000 tons of cement and petrol, respectively. The groundnut project mainly contributed to the railways' record profit in 1947 which was £318,493;[160] almost £290,000 was allocated to the Renewals Fund.

Meanwhile, the railways acquired sixteen American engines from the Malaya railways; six new British engines, and four locomotives from the Burmese Railways in addition to four Indian-built engines found lying idle at El Shatt, the British army depot in Egypt, from where the Tanganyika Railways bought 430 wagons. The substitution of worn-down stock was imperative for cost reasons and also for the increased demand by the groundnut scheme.[161]

---

[159] Lord Hailey, *An African Survey. A Study of Problems Arising in Africa South of the Sahara*. Revised 1956. Oxford 1957, pp.1294-6.
[160] Revenue amounted to £1,883,996 while expenditure stood at £1,252,298. Loan charges equalled £307,214.
[161] Hill, Permanent Way. Vol.II, pp.269-70.

One year later, the Tanganyika Railways was amalgamated with the Kenya and Uganda Railways in the wake of the East African Federation from which Great Britain, the imperial power, expected greater economic rewards. The Federation foreclosed the prospects of Tanganyika which became the auxiliary economy for Kenya.[162]

---

[162] The Federation "cannot be understood apart from the concurrent demand for a free hand in the local affairs of Kenya", D.S. Rothschild, *Towards Unity in Africa: A Study of Federalism in British Africa*. Washington, D.C., 1960, p.18.

4. Railway Organisation

Tanganyika Railways adopted the traditional departmental system that had been introduced by the British railways in the nineteenth century. Later, railways, however, opted for the divisional system. Train movement and traffic operation, running and maintenance of locomotives was combined into one department as happened with the other East African railways and elsewhere in British colonial Africa.[163] The various departments were managed and supervised by the Administration. The General Manager reported to the colonial government because "Tanganyika Railways is an integrated part of the Government and whilst for administrative and economic reasons its finances are separately managed it has no railway land or railway fund of its own. Its finances are incorporated into the Territory's account. It is directly controlled by Government through the Legislative Council. There is no possibility of its adopting a policy inimical to Government interests or against Government policy".[164]

To serve the interests of colonial capitalism Railway Administration favoured an Advisory Council that should advise on economic and financial matters.[165] For these reasons the Council on request by the colonial administration[166] was formed by representatives of the colony's leading entrepreneurs and industrial lobbies.[167] Even

---

[163] Hammond Report 1930, p.26.
[164] GMR to Chief Secretary, 22/05/1937: Memorandum on Advisory Council; TNA/S/R/ 20678.
[165] GMR to Chief Secretary, 18/01/1932; TNA/S/R/ 20678. The GMR "has no council before whom to lay his cases on finance, rates etc. and under a council should enable decisions in regards to rates etc. to be taken quickly. Similar to K.U.R. which the Chief Secretary mentioned when asking the GMR for his opinion on the Council."
[166] The proposals by the Railways focused on the following composition; cf. GMR to Chief Secretary, 15/04/1932; TNA/S/R/ 20678: Chief Secretary (chairman); Members: Director of Agriculture; Land Officer; Major Lead; Chairman, DSM Chamber of Commerce. GMR would attend meetings in an advisory capacity. This proposal was modified by colonial administration that insisted on a more business-oriented approach; cf. Chief Secretary, S.M.P. No. 20678/54, 4/05/1932; TNA/S/R/ 20678:
Chief Secretary as chairman; The Treasurer, Comptroller of Customs, Director of Agriculture, Major Lead, A.A. Adamjee (from Karimjee Jiranjee Co.), A.A. Brooks (Manager, National Bank of India), H.H. Robinson (Smith, Mackenzie and Co.).
[167] Tanganyika Coffee Growers' Assoc. asked to be represented at the Council; TCGA to Chief Secretary, 15/07/1936; TNA/S/R/ 20678. TCGA finally admitted but "used the Council as a forum in which they can endeavour to force certain sectional views which they have not been successful in pressing elsewhere"; GMR to Chief Secretary, 1/02/1937; TNA/S/R/ 20678.
Tanganyika Sisal Growers' Assoc. as represented by Mr. M.A. Carlson informed Colonial Officer about its railway policy. "In their view (a) he Advisory Council should increase its powers in decision-making and management and (b) that Tanganyika Railways should be transformed into a public company in which the Government would be the only shareholders"; Seel, Colonial Officer to Chief Secretary, 4/10/1944; TNA/S/R/ 20678.

later, representatives of the African proto-trade union, the Railway African Association [RAA], were not admitted. It was argued that "[t]he interests of the Africans working in the Tanganyika Railways and Ports Services are not properly safe-guarded as there is no African representative in the Railways Advisory Council. At a recent meeting the question was fully discussed, and I am directed by my Association to enquire whether the question of appointing an African representative to this Council could be considered by the Railways Administration".[168] To this Railways responded as follows: "It is not the function of the Railway Council to deal with matters relating to individual staff cases".[169] This answer could not satisfy the RAA. Eventually, the colonial administration intervened on behalf of the Railways and added: "It is noted in this connection that the terms of reference of the Civil Service exclude matters relating to Railway staff, and His Excellency would be glad if you would consider whether it is not advisable to establish a Railway Staff Board on similar lines".[170]

The internal division of operations is organised as follows. The Engineering and Locomotive Departments[171] cover infrastructure tasks while the Traffic Department looks after the operational side.[172] These departments are approached from a sociological position that should help the understanding of the workplace and the working conditions.

I.

The **Engineering Department** is in charge of maintenance and of new construction, survey and capital works.

The department maintains three districts, two on the Central Line and one on the Tanga Line with headquarters at Dar es Salaam, Tabora and Tanga. It is headed by the Chief Engineer whose main operative charge covers construction and survey. The Senior District Engineer acts as deputy for the Chief Engineer for maintenance work. The other senior officers include five District and 10 Assistant Engineers. The

---

[168] Ogilo, Hon.Sec. Railway African Association, to GMR, 13/11/1944; TNA/S/R/ 20678.
[169] GMR to RAA, 15/11/1944; TNA/S/R/ 20678.
[170] Chief Secretary to GMR, 27/02/1945; TNA/S/R/ 20678.
[171] as well as Ports Services. Because of the very distinct organisation, composition of work harbours must be treated as one separate entity.
[172] Accounting and Stores Department belong to this group, too. They are neglected in the further discussion.

latter two groups manage the operative supervision whose performance is delegated to European Inspectors of Works in each district. The senior departmental ranks are filled by Europeans.[173]

About permanent way, this function is carried out by Permanent Ways Inspectors [PWI] who also include some Indians. Each PWI is in charge of approximately 75 miles.[174] He has under him two or three Sub.PWIs, either Indian or African. The single Sub.PWI co-ordinates five gangs consisting of 12 persons. On average, each gang is in charge of five miles. The PWI controls the track once on a weekly basis while the Sub.PWI inspects the track twice a week whereby each gang is controlled four times a week.[175] This system adopted from the Indian Railways " appears to suit the local conditions".[176]

The controlling system is executed by the Chief Engineer who after the annual estimates are approved makes the definite fund allocation to the various districts. "The District Engineer controls the expenditure on a monthly basis and reports to the Chief Engineer who knows by the 8th of the month the current expenditure."[177]

In the early twenties, the number of maintenance sections amounted to 12 on the Central Line and 4 on the Tanga Line with an average length of 100 Kms. The section: Dar es Salaam-Itigi reported to the headquarters at Dodoma, the Itigi-Kigoma to Tabora, and the Tabora-Mwanza to Shinyanga.[178]

The number of trackmen was 1.27 persons per Km on the Central Line and 1.32 on the Tanga Line, in 1923.[179] The number of trackmen was further reduced in 1924 to 1.12 on the Central Line, but increased to 1.54 on the Tanga Line.[180] However, the number of trackmen on the Central Line was augmented and reached 2.54 in

---

[173] Hammond Report 1930, p.12.
[174] In the wake of the Great Depression this rank was almost totally staffed by Indians for reasons of low wages. In order to maintain a high performance level the new posts of District Permanent Way Inspector was introduced what implied the re-composition of work among the upper European ranks without inflicting additional costs; see Tanganyika Railways, Annual Report, 1932, p.8.
[175] In 1938, the staff at inspector level consisted of 80 men: 12 European PWIs, 7 Indian PWIs, and 2 African PWIs in addition to 2 Junior PWIs. 57 Sub.PWIs of whom 51 Africans completed the operative top; Tanganyika Railways, Annual Report, 1938, p.38.
[176] Hammond Report 1930, p.8.
[177] Hammond Report 1930, p.9.
[178] Hammond Report 1930, p.7.
[179] Chief Engineer Annual Report, 1923, p.11.
[180] Chief Engineer Annual Report, 1924, p.8.

1929.[181] Besides, the economic depression in the early thirties led to sharp cuts in personnel so that the trackmen were reduced to 1.44 per Km.[182]

The reduncanies effected safety and efficiency as was acknowledged by the official report for 1934.[183] After the economic recovery the employment figures slightly increased as follows:

District	Number of employed	Open lines in Km	Men per Km
Dodoma	1,170	741	1.6
Tabora	1,429	1,036	1.4
Tanga Line	711	438	1.6
Total	3,310	2,215	1.5

Source: Tanganyika Railways, Annual Report, 1937, p.43.

By 1940, the trackmen per Km had been cut to 1.26; this reduction, obviously for cost reasons, was accompanied from the increase of temporary labour that accounted for 0.50 in the same year.[184] By this measure, cost per kilometre was cut from £35.65 in 1937 to £34.96 in nominal prices.[185] War-induced inflation, however, led to rising costs that amounted to £42.77 for 1947, the railways' last year of autonomy.[186]

Construction of new railway lines, and the relaying of worn-down tracks form the second task to be performed by the Department. As the construction works are discussed in the context of African labour a summary seems sufficient at this stage.

In 1923, the extension of the Tanga Line from Moshi to the Sanya River, on the way to Arusha, started. The extension was about 22 miles in length.[187] The work was completed in December 1925.[188]

The Tabora-Mwanza line was begun in early 1926. In that year only 103 kilometres could be completed due to heavy rains.[189] The cost estimates as having were considered by the loan application run at £657,000.[190] The construction of the 232

---
[181] Hammond Report 1930, p.8.
[182] Tanganyika Railways, Annual Report, 1932, p.8. One year later, the maintenance staff was further reduced to 1.3 men per Km; Report for 1933, p.14.
[183] General Manager Report, 1934, p.16.
[184] General Manager Report, 1940, p.46.
[185] General Manager Report, 1941, p.5.
[186] General Manager Report, 1947, p.12.
[187] Tanganyika Railways, Annual Report, 1923, p.1.
[188] Tanganyika Railways, Annual Report, 1924/5, p.9.
[189] Tanganyika Railways, Annual Report, 1925/6; General Manager Report, 1925/6, p.1.
[190] General Manager Report, 1925/6, p.5.

route miles was completed in mid-1928.[191] One year later, the Moshi-Arusha extension opened to the public traffic. This line of 53 miles in length passes by the Kahé junction that connects the Tanganyika system to the Kenya and Uganda Railways.[192]

Without a Construction Branch at the Engineering Department the new lines have been built by local firms under contract. However, the Chief Engineer and the General Manager both favoured the future construction to be carried out by the Department. This includes the extension planning that was decided in the late twenties with an eye on deploying the railways as vehicle for economic development of the Southern Highlands.[193]

The next construction work was the Manyoni branch line from the Central Line to Kinyangiri by way of Singida, a total of 150 Kms. The project approved in 1930 was contracted to a Kenyan firm.[194] At the height of the economic depression, the contract rates "represent a very marked drop from those customary in this Territory during the last five or six years.[...] They will have to be very carefully watched and it is by non means certain that they can be kept at their present low level once the territory's trade and industry recovers".[195]

In the same year the railway reconstruction of the Central Line between Kidete and Godegode started. The work shifted the track from the valley ground to the slopes hereby avoiding the previous floods, debris fans and flood silt. The task was performed by the same construction company that had been the contractor of the Tabora-Mwanza branch line. It covered 31 Kms in length with estimated costs of £7,800 per km or approximately £242,000 in total. Because of the difficult terrain and the heavy protective works at the Romuma River bridge the work made necessary almost 18 months before completion.[196]

Lastly, the railway commissioned the relaying of track through the Usinge Swamp. To safeguard against a future submerging of the main line the track bank was raised along 8 kilometres. The cost amounted to £14,000.[197]

The Kidete and Usinge reconstruction works were completed in 1932.[198] That these tasks were started at the height of the economic depression simply follows from

---

[191] Tanganyika Railways, Annual Report, 1929, p.6.
[192] Hammond Report 1930, p.4.
[193] This position was rejected for costs and efficiency; see Hammond Report 1930, p.11.
[194] Tanganyika Railways, Annual Report, 1930, p.6.
[195] Tanganyika Railways, Annual Report, 1931, p.2.
[196] Tanganyika Railways, Annual Report, 1932, p.2.
[197] Tanganyika Railways, Annual Report, 1932, p.2.
[198] Tanganyika Railways, Annual Report, 1932, p.4.

the modalities of fund allocation as the projects had been submitted and approved before. Any delay or withdrawal would not only have resulted in the loss of funds but also would have cancelled any future efforts for the same projects. It, however, would be misleading to identify the capital spending as an effort by the railways for economic stimulation. The work primarily was based on contract labour with barely any inputs concerning the Tanganyika industries. Also, the funds were too small for any significant contribution to economic improvement.

After the completion of the Manyoni branch line in 1932, all new construction works came to a complete halt for four years. It was only in 1936 that capital works at a very small-scale were re-started.[199] This pattern persisted until 1945.

Regarding minor capital works of relaying an almost identical picture persists. Track relaying, primarily, is necessary for traffic safety. In the context of the Tanganyika Railways a second factor has to be taken into account.

The German-built railways served military purposes and strategic options what explains that the track of the Central Line could not carry heavy loads; also, it was hastily built and therefore needed frequent repair works. Through relaying the track was adjusted to heavier loading capacity and greater train frequency. Thus, in 1923 a total of 61.9 Kms of the Central Line was re-laid.[200] During the following two years relaying of another 132 Kms was performed.[201] Until 1930, the entire track of the Tanga Line had been re-laid with 45 lb.sleepers[202] that substituted the light German 31 lb. permanent way. By that year the total relaying work of the Territory's railway system was completed whereby a high standard was achieved according to General Hammond's analysis.[203] For this reason and for the financial constraints in the wake of the economic depression relaying become a minor activity in the thirties.

The annual expenditure reflects these trends; whereas the cost amounted to £119,606 in 1930 it, successively, was reduced to £83,387 in 1941 what equalled the cost reduction per km by almost one quarter.[204]

---

[199] General Manager Report, 1936, p.39.
[200] Tanganyika Railways, Annual Report, 1923, p.13.
[201] General Manager Report, 1925, p.1.
[202] Tanganyika Railways, Annual Report, 1930, p.10.
[203] Hammond Report 1930, p.4.
[204] General Manager Report, 1934, p.16; 1942, p.6.

The Department, the second largest in employment terms at the railways, had a staff of 3,585 persons in 1923 of which 36 Europeans, 54 Indians, and 3,495 Africans. The latter group was composed as follows:

Occupation	Number of Total	As Percentage
Clerks	11	0.30
Draftsmen	2	0.05
Sub. Perm.Way Inspectors	29	0.80
Gangers/ Trackmen	2,167	62.05
Other Labour	916	26.20
Capital & Loan Labour *	370	10.60
Total	3,495	100.00

Annotation: * Workers for track relaying and construction, along with contract labour employed by construction companies.

Source: Chief Engineer's Statistical Tables, Supplement to Annual Report 1923, p.3.

The composition reveals that Africans filled the lowest ranks and were employed for unskilled tasks. The Department, therefore, exactly mirrors the colonial economy.

Until the Great Depression the employment numbers increased to 6,139 of which 5,943 Africans. The necessary cost reduction exercises translated into major employment cuts so that by 1936 the staff stood at 4,405 of which 4,314 Africans; the cuts also effected the higher ranks occupied by Europeans and Indians. The cheaper African labour substituted the ranks previously held by Indians whose employment figure shows a decline from 138 to 53 in 1936.[205] The employment situation persisted in spite of the colony's economic recovery so that in 1941 the Department's staff numbered 4,359 of which 4,276 Africans.[206] The requirements of Britain at war led to an increase of employment. In 1945, employment amounted to 5,713 of which 5,623 Africans. This trend persisted in the wake of the post-war development scheme and stood at 7,930 (Africans employment figure: 7,346) at the eve of the merger with the K.U.R. system in 1947.[207]

II.

The **Locomotive Department** is in charge of the railways' locomotives and the running stock. This task requires workshops for maintenance and repair.

---

[205] Tanganyika Railways, Annual Report, 1930, p.85; General Manager Report, 1936, p.48.
[206] General Manager Report, 1941, p.55.
[207] General Manager Report, 1947, p.3.

Maintenance and repair needed heavy machinery. The installation was capital intensive what explains the inflexible structure of the department in comparison to the Engineering Department. It also explains that the organisational structure as was inherited from the Germans had to be maintained. The *Kolonialbahnen* had built three separate workshops at Dar es Salaam and Tabora on the Central Line and at Tanga. Intention had been to establish the main workshops of the Central Line at Tabora with the gradual abolition of the Dar es Salaam shop. In consequence with the military strategy of the railway construction the Tabora workshop was the most modern and best equipped.

The British colonial administration identified Dar es Salaam as the administrative and economic centre so that the Tanganyika Railways neglected Tabora for Dar es Salaam. Because of the excellent equipment the Tabora workshop continued to preserve its performance at a high standard even though no further investment was done.

An almost similar situation existed for the Tanga workshops where the railway policy was "to spend as little on workshops as was compatible with keeping the current work going".[208]

This policy takes the non-economical structure into consideration that it intends to change gradually through the investment focus on Dar es Salaam.

The Department's policy must be understood against this particular background.

Concerning organisation the department is divided into three districts each with its workshops. Each district is headed by a District Locomotive Superintendent. He is assisted from an Assistant Locomotive Superintendent who manages the workshops. The running section is supervised by the District Officer.

The District reports to the Chief Mechanical Engineer and his senior staff of one Assistant Locomotive Superintendent and one Technical Assistant. The Department's executive level, therefore, consists of eleven persons.[209]

The locomotives, their number and working quality, condition the Department's work besides the rolling stock. Therefore, the development of equipment precedes the discussion of the workshops.

---

[208] Hammond Report 1930, p.13.
[209] Hammond Report 1930, p.13.

The Tanganyika Railways took over from the *Kolonialbahnen*. Because of the financial constraints to which Britain had been exposed after the armistice the railways could not immediately substitute the fleet of worn-down German engines. It took more than ten years before the process of modernisation was completed:

Description of Locomotives	No. in 1923	No. in 1930	No. in 1940
GERMAN ENGINES			
- Goods	23	17	-
- Tanks	26	12	3
- Mallet Class	8	-	-
- S Class	1	1	-
- Shunting Tank	6	6	-
BOUGHT AFTER 1918			
- D.L.Class (UK)	6	6	6
- F.Class (Indian)	13	3	-
- G.Class (")	4	-	-
- G.Class (") Nizam	4	13	17
- M.Class (")	3	-	-
- M.K.Class (UK)	-	11	11
- B.Class (Uganda R.)	1	-	-
- R.V.Class (UK)	-	5	11
- Shunting Engine (")	1	-	-
- Shunting Tank (UK)	-	-	12
- Sentinel Shunting (TR)	-	1	-
- other	-	-	3
Total	96	75	63

Sources: Chief Mechanical Engineer Report, 1923, pp.26ff; Tanganyika Railways, Annual Report, 1930, p.81; 1940, p.47.

The preceding statistics portray various elements; the complete substitution of German engines follows from the total depreciation for technical reasons while the reduction of engines observes the increasing efficiency. The tractive capacity was drastically improved; the R.V. Class engines had a joint capacity of 309,320 lb. (1940) with three engines of more than 40,000 lb. tractive power each. The same refers to the medium-sized Nizams whose number was increased as well.

Finally, the modern fleet required less maintenance beyond routine works and provided a greater running performance.

The rolling stock was improved and modernised parallel to the engine development. In 1940 the 1,163 goods wagons had a total carrying capacity of 13,138 tons. Coaching vehicles amounted to 228 units with 2,200 seats.[210]

---

[210] Tanganyika Railways, Annual Report, 1940, p.49.

The Department's Locomotive Section also was responsible for watering arrangements, fuel and lubrication. Among these operative tasks watering and fuels were the most problematic for reasons of adequate supplies.

Particularly on the Central Line that passes through Tanganyika's semi-arid central plateau water posed a permanent problem. The engines ran on wood fuel. Without local coal deposits wood fuel was the most economical alternative which Britain followed.

The steam engines' boilers needed frequent watering what depended on the carrying load. For climatic reasons the water tanks had to be filled up before the passage through the semi-arid country-side what reduces the commercial carrying load.[211] To make matters worse, water remains scarce along the entire track for most of the dry season.[212] These difficulties mainly refer to the situation of the Central Line. As the watering stations are located at the main railway stations the "town demands at all places have increased and frequently this reacts on the amount available for locomotive purposes".[213]

The official analysis for 1930 aptly describes the persistent difficulties: "Water supplies again caused trouble; there were partial failures at Ngerengere, Kidete, Humwa, Dodoma, and Tabora, and total failures at Kikombo, Nzinge, Tura, Nyahua, and Lugufu. Another source of trouble is the large percentage of liquid mud in some of the supplies on the Central Line, which makes it difficult to keep the boilers clean and to prevent them from priming.[214]

This situation persisted throughout the economic depression. The General Manager's Report for 1934, therefore, concluded that "particularly on the 700 kilometres plateau section of the Central Line, on 300 kilometres of its branches, and on the semi-desert section from Buiko to Kahe on the Tanga Line. That this state of affairs will become much more serious if and when the hoped for traffic increase takes place, is obvious".[215]

---

[211] For the Morogoro-Itigi section on the Central Line auxiliary water tanks had to be attached to the locomotives; Chief Mechanical Engineer Report, 1923, p.19.
[212] Hammond Report 1930, p.16.
[213] Chief Mechanical Engineer Report, 1924, p.14. Even worse, Water scarcity resulted in conflicts with the peasants of the Pare Mountains, "a further sign, in the words of the General Manager, that these denuded hills will not much longer provide the necessary water for both the population and the railway"; General Manager Report, 1934, p.27.
[214] Tanganyika Railways, Annual Report, 1930, p.10.
[215] General Manager Report, 1934, p.27.

In the coming years the Department improved the situation through the installation of steam pumping and electrical pumps. By 1939, 65 pumps were in use that rendered the water supply more reliable.[216]

The water scarcity, however, remained a bottleneck for efficient railway operations particularly in the context of increasing traffic.

The fuel situation was somewhat different. Wood fuelling followed from the lack of local coal deposits. The Tanganyika Railways reconsidered the use of wood once the economic recovery started. At some sections of the Central Line fuel wood became scarce and more expensive while coal promised a more economical alternative particularly if the engines run under full capacity. Also the modern locomotives that substituted the old German engines showed a higher energy output when fired with coal.

The Department began to import South African coal in 1924. By 1930, the Dar es Salaam-Morogoro and Tanga-Buiko sections used coal because the wood fuel price exceeded the upper limit of Shs.11.30 per 100 cu.ft. It has to be added that wood supplies were contracted to private companies what left the Department with little margins in cost management terms.[217]

At the end of the decade almost half of the railways' engine fleet operated on coal.[218] Notably the powerful goods engines (Nizams and G class) had been converted to coal. However, wood fuel continued to play a minor role primarily for reasons of economies in regions with sufficient and cheap wood supplies.

On average, the section accounted for 25 per cent of the Department's costs with fuel consuming almost 17 per cent of the total. Against this background the experiments with alternative supplies must be seen.[219]

The railways inherited three workshops, two on the Central Line at Tabora and Dar es Salaam, and at Tanga for the Tanga Line.

---

[216] General Manager Report, 1939, p.42.
[217] Hammond Report 1930, p.14.
[218] On the Tanga Line, wood fuel was used only in locomotives for lighting up; cf. General Manager Report, 1936, p.31.
[219] By 1939, the annual expenditure for fuel, related to identical engine mileage, was reduced to £24,800 from the previous £34,000, the average amount in the late twenties/early thirties; cf. General Manager Report, 1939, p.91, Table 15(b).

As usual, the shops were in charge of engine and rolling stock maintenance, repair, and general overhaul.[220] The engineering works required capital-intensive heavy equipment such as pits, cranes, and foundries. It follows that for reasons of optimal capacity utilisation the shops accepted orders from other railway departments as well as from the colony's private industries.

In the twenties, the Dar es Salaam workshops were modernised[221] with the Tabora shops being maintained at approximately the same level of equipment that the Germans had installed. The Dar es Salaam shops included five pits; of these one was required for light repairs and one for tenders while the remaining three pits were available for general overhauls and erections.[222] At Tanga, no improvements were made apart from a few machine tools. The lack of capacity extension and modernisation resulted in operational bottlenecks to which added the work orders by the sisal plantations. Being the only mechanical workshop in the northern part of the colony the Tanga shops had to perform urgent repairs to the sisal industry's heavy machinery, the major customer of the Railways. During the twenties this policy stemmed from the uncertainty of the Tanga Line that was targeted for the take-over by the Kenya Railways. During and after the economic depression the Railways lacked the funds for capital extension works at Tanga that had to cope with the uneconomical situation.[223]

Because of financial constraints the Railways had to operate the German locomotives what explain the heavy repair works in spite of the low traffic.[224]

The economic depression after 1930 effected the workshops in various ways. First, for economies the Tabora shops were closed down in 1931. Future works were carried out in the Dar es Salaam shop. Only minor repair works such as the overhauls of four-wheel stock were performed at the Tabora sheds. Second, a system of progressing locomotive repairs through shops was started in 1931, and resulted in

---

[220] Repair works fall under three categories. As for locomotives heavy repairs cover complete repair to engine and boiler. Boilers are removed from frame, and engines are lifted. Medium repairs extend to complete repair to engines and to light repairs to boilers and mountings. Light repairs equal general overhaul of engine. For coaching vehicles and wagons only two repair categories are applicable. Heavy repairs include general repairs to bodies and underframes that also consider wheels, drawgear, and brakes. Light repairs cover all other repair works such as varnishing and lifting.
[221] Modernisation included a new boiler shop, one smith shop, and one foundry; this work was completed in 1927; cf. Report on Tanganyika Territory, 1927, (Col.32), p.46.
[222] Hammond Report 1930, p.18.
[223] Hammond Report 1930, p.18; Tanganyika Railways, Annual Report, 1940, p.11.
[224] The Tanganyika Railways, Annual Report, 1930, p.11, states that because of "the old German engines maintenance and repair costs becomes heavier and heavier each year, and more difficult to keep them in service. These engines accounted for 54.7 percent of the total failures on the combined lines".

locomotives being given a general overhaul in Dar es Salaam in fifty working days.[225] Third, the Dar sheds were reorganised with the following objectives: to perform heavy repairs to a locomotive within fifty working days; to increase the daily repair works for goods vehicles to three units per day including spray painting and numbering; to cut the workshop labour force in accordance with the reduced locomotive 'out-turn'.[226] If avoidable, heavy repairs were cut down while the remaining labour force was put on daily rates of cut down pay. Thus, the working expenditure was reduced by approximately one third.[227]

While railway traffic remained low because of the protracted economic recovery Administration considered further cost reduction measures. Thus, the maximum period in service between general repairs extended from 3 to 5 years based on an optimum engine mileage between the shedding period of 160.000 kilometres. This decision, effective from 1936, was accompanied from the introduction of 'service repair' that covered all work necessary to the proper maintenance of an engine during its service period. The objectives of these measures were evident. It was hoped that the Dar es Salaam workshops would perform the repair works on the basis of the previous cost reduction without aflicting delays. It was expected that the service repair would contribute as it should secure the proper running of the locomotives even under conditions of the extended service period.

But the workshops' production design was inflexible for reasons of necessary machinery equipment and trained personnel. Therefore, the workshop was forced into work contracts with Government Departments and private industries.[228]

The war economy, however, changed the policy. Traffic increased considerably and affected the workshops accordingly. But the increased work load could not be handled properly owing to the lack of experienced staff. In other words, the workshops had to cope with these deficits in a very unsatisfactory way. It can be argued that the war economy was not predictable so that planning for sustained capacity increase was not feasible.

Notwithstanding these considerations, the pre-war capacity reduction in combination with the extended locomotive service period would have led to a similar constel-

---

[225] Tanganyika Railways, Annual Report, 1931, p.21.
[226] Tanganyika Railways, Annual Report, 1932, p.13.
[227] Tanganyika Railways, Annual Report, 1932, p.21.
[228] The workshops performed the manufacturing of engine parts and rough castings. The value of contracts for private industry approximated £3,500 in the pre-war years, and reached £13,000 p.a. during the war. This increase identified the effects of import substitution. Roughly ¾ of the works went to Railway and Government Departments; cf. Tanganyika Railways, Annual Report, 1939, p.38; 1941, p.11.

lation at a later stage. While in 1930 the average total engine mileage amounted to 1,485,000 kilometres it increased to 1,637,000 kilometres in 1941 and to 2,279,000 kilometres in 1945. As the locomotive stock remained unaltered the respective traffic load increased considerably[229] that caused the rapid decline in train kilometres per engine failure from 162,226 kilometres in 1935 to 15,140 kilometres in 1942. Also, the annual repair works carried out reflects on this development as shown by the following table:

Year	Dar es Salaam Heavy	Med.	Light	Er.	Tabora Heavy	Medium	Light	Tanga Heavy	Med.	Light	Er.
1923	5	2	-		4	1	5	4	1	5	
1924	4	5	1		10	-	5	3	2	1	
1930	5	6	3		5	4	5	5	2	3	
1935	10	2	4		closed			3	1	-	
1936	11	1	5					3	-	-	
1939	7	4	1					1	2	1	1
1942	7	6	2					3	-	-	2
1947	10	8	4.5	9				3	1	17	-
1948	5.5.	11	10.5	10.5				5	-	44	-

Annotations: Med. = Medium; Er. = Erection works (after 1939)

Sources: Tanganyika Railways, Annual Report, 1923, p.31; 1924, p.19; 1930, p.84; 1935, p.15; 1936, p.35; 1941, p.42; 1942, p.43; 1948, p.170.

In the pre-war period the ratio of average repair volume to locomotive stock equalled 29 per cent in the Dar es Salaam shops while during the war this ratio declined to 24 per cent. However, due to service delays the repair-to-stock ratio increased dramatically to 70 per cent.

The traffic requirements put further pressure on the workshops to shorten the time under repair. Thus, from an average of 79 days in the early thirties repair time was reduced to 54.2 days during the war that guaranteed the full capacity use of the shops. In 1942, for example, locomotive and wagon repairs extended to 1387 days out of a total working volume for five pits of 1550 days. To this must be added war production that although not detailed covered a considerable amount of time. Production mainly included cylinders, pistons and river pontoons.[230]

---

[229] In the mid-thirties the average annual service mileage per locomotive came to 25,000 kilometres or 125,000 kilometres if the five-year service period is considered. Ten years later the respective figures stood at 37,000 kilometres per year or 184,000 kilometres for the length of service period. According to official estimates the locomotives could run a service period of 160-180,000 kilometres without inflicting any damage to engines and boilers. Translated into the war conditions the Railways deliberately took serious risks as locomotives operated beyond the technical optimum.
[230] Tanganyika Railways, Annual Report, 1946, p.3.

Employment is structured by the work requirements that fall under the categories of locomotive running and repairing. It follows that the various work tasks demand basic technical skills and artisan skills, as well. Moreover, the work requires a strict time management for the locomotive to run on schedule and a team-oriented performance in the repair shops. The colonial appearance makes itself felt in the general division of labour whereby the supervisory tasks are monopolised by European engineers and managers while the lower grades are contested by Indian and African workers. Employment policy aims at the substitution of higher paid Indians from Africans.

The extended railway network, on the one hand, and the climatic and geographical stress on the running equipment, on the other, explains that the Department is the second-largest unit in employment terms.[231]

The next tables portray the staff development according to ethnicity:

Year	Europeans	Indians	Africans unspecified	skilled	unskilled
1920	N.a.	584		451	N.a.
1921	N.a.	416		481	N.a.
1922	N.a.	437		617	N.a.
1923	53	381		659	882
1924	50	382	1,487		
1925	55	392	1,796		
1926	61	432	1,891		
1927	72	407	2,179		
1928	73	453	2,355		
1929	76	471	2,240		
1930	79	433	2,204		
1931	89	456	2,342		
1932	47	157	1,579		
1933	47	155	1,461		
1934	44	154	1,454		
1935	40	179	1,477		
1936	41	173	1,441		
1937	41	163	1,441		
1938	38	166	1,387		
1939	36	156	1,403		
1940	36	181	2,165		
1941	34	184	2,743		
1942	36	206	3,778		
1946	42	248	2,097	1,493	604
1947	45	174	2,521	1,662	859

Sources: Tanganyika Railways, Annual Report, 1923, p.33; 1924, p.25; 1925, p.47; 1926, p.58; 1927, p.57; 1928, p.54; 1929, p.66; 1930, p.85; 1931, p.72; 1933, p.57; 1935, p.56; 1936, p.48; 1937, p.119; 1939, p.139; 1941, p.55; 1942, p.54; 1947, p.80.

---

[231] In 1923 the Engineering Department employed 3,889 men of which 3,811 African workers; until 1930 the staff increased to 6,139 and 5,943, respectively. Under the impact of the economic crisis and the retarded recovery the staff number was reduced to 5,327 and 5,229 in 1939; General Manager Report, 1923, p.64; 1939, p.139; Chief Accountant Report 1923/24, p.25; 1924/25, p.47; Tanganyika Railways, Annual Report, 1930, p.85; 1932, p.74.

The preceding table shows how Railway Administration adjusted employment to the economic cycle. It becomes apparent that the lower works as being occupied by Africans were the most effected from redundancy. On the other, manual and unskilled labour was recruited once the economic upspring required fresh labour. However, management requirements augmented as well. In 1923 one manager supervised 29.08 lower grade workers; this ratio changed to 33.60 during the economic depression and was intensified under the war economy where it reached 60.14. Finally, the trend into substitution of Indian labour for African is clearly discernible: In the beginning of operations, Tanganyika Railways employed one Indian worker for four African labourers. This ratio altered to 1:10 in the thirties, and to 1:8.3 during the war. The substitution follows economies because African labour obviously is much cheaper. As the Indians occupied skilled jobs the substitution trend also outlines the training policy pursued by the Railways.

In the early twenties Tanganyika Railways employed 20 African locomotive drivers and shunters along with 108 Locomotive stokers. In the years to come these numbers improved to 44 and 123, respectively.[232] Also, the number of trained artisans increased to more than 400.[233] This increase must be placed against the background of employment policy and the African training schemes what will be discussed at later stage.

III.

The **Traffic Department** forms the commercial link of the Railways that includes all transactions with the public regarding coaching and goods. In addition, it is in charge of the train movements and of staff supervision at stations, in the trains, and along the railway lines.[234]

---

[232] In 1936, African drivers formed 56 percent of the total employed; Tanganyika Railways, Annual Report, 1936, p.35.
[233] Tanganyika Railways, Annual Report, 1923, p.15; 1934, p.29.
[234] According to Hammond Report 1930, p.6. The department is also in charge of the traffic on Lake Tanganyika.

The department is organised in three districts, two on the Central Line with headquarters at Dar es Salaam and Tabora, and one on the Tanga Line with headquarters at Tanga.[235]

In principle, the department's performance depended on the general economic situation that formed the major factor in the Railways' matrix of profits. To this added the departmental policy of cost management; capacity utilisation increase; and productivity increase at handling sides.

The commercial policy formed one important vector in the Railways' financial matrix that contributed to the objective of economic development under colonialism. The state-owned Railways reacted to government policy that it translated into economic practice. The General Manager adjusted policy priorities to the Railways' financial feasibility what defined his major strategic task that, in turn, conditioned the Traffic Department. For these reasons, commercial policy of the Traffic Department is approached under operational aspects while broader implications will be discussed in the context of the Railways' management and economic policy.

Commercial success depended on an adequate infrastructure of train operations, cargo handling, and passenger service. Since 1923 the Railways operated its goods and passenger traffic as follows:[236]

A. Train Service on Central Line:

(1) Regular service for mixed goods trains
    1 Mail Train   }
    1 Mixed Train } Up and Down between DSM and Kigoma
    1 Goods Train }
    1 Goods Train   Up and Down between DSM and Tabora

(2) Goods trains run as required on the Central Line.
    The majority of export cargo consisted of peasant produce that explains why the Railways had to adjust traffic to the crop season. On average, during the months of July to September, 500 special goods trains were deployed, and approximately 200 on the Tabora-Mwanza branch line for the same purpose.[237]

(3) Working Time Table

    DSM-Morogoro (202 km): 10 Up and Down trains per week
    M'goro-Dodoma (255 km): 10 Up and Down trains per week
    Dodoma-Itigi   (169 km): 8 Up and Down trains per week
    Itigi-Tabora   (214 km): 7 Up and Down trains per week
    Tabora-Kigoma (410 km): 5 Up and Down trains per week[238]

---

[235] Hammond Report 1930, p.22.
[236] Tanganyika Railways, Annual Report, 1923, p.38.
[237] General Manager Report, 1936, p.28.
[238] Reduced to two trains per week in 1927 due to small passenger traffic; Tanganyika Railways, Annual Report, 1927/28, p.103.

B. Train Service on Tanga Line:

1 Mail   Up and Down between Tanga and Moshi per week
1 Mixed Up and Down between Tanga and Korogwe (5 days in the week)
1 Mixed Up and Down between Tanga and Buiko (1 day in the week)

C. Train Service on Branch Lines:

The passenger traffic service on the new branch lines was un-economical:

"Trains to and from Mwanza were only feasible during and just after the produce season when money is circulating more freely and many natives might like to travel to Mwanza to do their shopping. [Because of the time-table] there is no time to transact any business before the return train leaves. Even coming in on Monday they do not always find time to transact their business and load goods in time to catch the train on Monday afternoon."[239] Therefore, the local trade community relied on traffic by lorry.

The Manyoni-Kinyangiri branch line was operated by a weekly mixed train as the reason for this line was the stimulation of peasant export production such as groundnuts and hides. Also, it should serve the newly discovered gold mines of the Mkalama District.[240]

Cargo handling required the co-ordination and control of rolling stock at the respective stations. Identification of free capacity under conditions of cost management led to the following reporting system for the Central Line.[241] Initially, stock reports were despatched by way of the trunk telegraph wire from all stations to district headquarters at 6 p.m. every evening. The Traffic Superintend at Tabora issued orders for working and distribution to the various stations. Parallel to it, Tabora informed Dar es Salaam office that either rectified the orders or adjusted them to the own arrangements.[242] This co-ordination system was centralised in 1927. Henceforth, the Traffic Manager's Office in Dar es Salaam managed the ordering of trains and the rolling stock distribution.[243] In the wake of the economic depression the traffic office at Tabora was closed that resulted in the direct reporting to Dar es Salaam.[244]

Traffic infrastructure relied on stations. The Railways opened 111 stations in the twenties. However, under the impact of the economic depression some 40 stations were closed. Passengers and goods traffic were excepted at the former stations by guards of train. Also, the sidings between stations enabled the loading/unloading of goods before special arrangements.[245] In spite of increased traffic during the war years the number of operating stations remained unchanged.

---

[239] Provincer, Lake Province to Traffic Manager, DSM, 19th Dec., 1934; TNA/S/R/ 12857.
[240] General Manager Report, 1932, p.10.
[241] The identical system was adopted on the Tanga Line where the stations reported to Tanga office.
[242] Hammond Report 1930, p.22.
[243] Tanganyika Railways, Annual Report, 1927/28, p.103.
[244] General Manager Report, 1935, p.12.
[245] General Manager Report, 1937, p.34. The total number of stations was as follows

The attraction of traffic depended on compatible tariff rates that must be seen as the Traffic Department's commercial tool. Even though the Railways enjoyed a logistical monopoly in many regions of the colony it faced heavy competition particularly in the most productive areas. For reasons of colonial valorisation the Kilimanjaro region became the first economic growth pole based on coffee cultivation and mixed settler farming. Exportation could either be directed to Mombasa or Tanga what explains the pre-eminent role of tariff rates. Along with the Kenya railways road traffic was a serious competitor for high valued commodities. It must be added that Mombasa's deep water port excelled in costs and time against the lighterage facilities at Tanga harbour.

On the Central Line this competition did not exist, at first glimpse. But, the majority of cargo handling came from the transit traffic with the Belgian Congo where alternative routes existed. Again, the Tanganyika Railways' attraction rested on tariff rates that rendered this route more economical than any alternative. Finally, the railway link with the prospering Lake Victoria basin must be approached from the same perspective. Trade could follow the alternative route by way of the Kenyan railway system.

Regarding the non-contested areas the Railways had to observe the ratio of freight costs to the marketable price. It is obvious that commodity marketing would be frustrated by high freight charges. Sisal seemed to constitute the exception as the plantations depended on the Railways' bulk-carrying capacity. The importance of sisal for the colony's economy for exports and employment rendered plantation capital a strong bargaining position that translated into preferential tariff rates.[246]

For these reasons, the Railways could not pursue a tariff policy of revenue optimisation. Passenger traffic was less important in revenue terms because of the low income level. Africans used the Railways only when necessary. Wealthy Europeans,

	Central Line	Tanga Line
Open	44	28
Closed	39	1
Sidings	15	12
Total	98	41

Sources: General Manager Report, 1931, p.9; 1937, p.34.
[246] Next to transit traffic sisal was the most important commodity followed from groundnuts, grown at Manyoni and Dodoma along the Central Line and along the Mwanza branch line; coffee remained contested by the Tanganyika and Kenya railway systems; Hammond Report 1930, pp.4-5.

however, relied on the Railways during the rainy season only and preferred their cars whenever feasible.

Dependence on transit traffic and sharp competition with other carriers for lucrative cargo in the territory's most advanced farming areas reduced the Railways' sphere of logistical monopoly to the minor commodity producing areas. Moreover, the economic composition of colonial capitalism founded the export orientation that conditioned the very restricted inter-territorial exchange of commodities.

Furthermore, the colony's economic policy prohibited any trade imbalances what pegged the value of imports to export earnings. Imports were directed to the most advanced regions where the same pattern that conditioned export trades prevailed.

The resulting precarious structure[247] made its full impact during the economic depression.

Until the outbreak of crisis the transit traffic with the Congo contributed almost fifty per cent of the Railways' revenue. This traffic was pivotal for another reason, too: "Congo traffic is vital to the welfare of the Railway. With the exception of the salt trade from Nyanza, it is the only traffic which passes over the long section of the Central Line from Usoke (Km 901) to Kigoma (Km 1,244), the fly belt and the large district of Ujiji producing practically nothing in the way of trade or traffic".[248]

An agreement with Union Minière du Haut-Katanga, the Congolese mining company, regulated the weekly transport of 210 tons copper and 60 tons tin-ore per month. Because of favourable tariff rates Congolese imports were directed towards the Tanganyika Railways, too. At the same time, this agreement reduced the operative costs because "[e]mpty haulage of vehicles, a distance of 1,245 Kms (DSM to Kigoma) is now being considerably reduced by the import of railway and tramway material, building material, cement, galvanised iron, and other material requiring the use of open wagons for transport to the Congo. [...] traffic in the up direction is increasing, whereas previously traffic was almost entirely restricted to the downward direction to DSM".[249]

Congolese copper exports climbed from 8,739 tons in 1924 to 33,329 tons in 1930 based on a freight rate of £3/10 per ton. Under the impact of the global crisis these

---

[247] As is acknowledged by the following statement of the General Manager: "The difficulty of running a Railway for a purely agricultural country is well known, and it seems that only the finding of minerals (copper, tin, coal, etc.) can hope to put the railway on a commercially sound basis of a permanent nature"; General Manager Report, 1924/25, p.3. This statement characterised not only the contemporary situation but also the future.
[248] General Manager Report, 1923, p.4.
[249] Tanganyika Railways, Annual Report, 1923, p.36.

exports contracted very sharply in 1931 when not more than 7,166 tons were handled.[250] Parallel to it, Congolese imports declined as well.[251] For the Railways the decrease of approximately 50,000 tons brought a revenue loss of £180,000. "Whereas in 1930-31 Congo traffic accounted for 48.97 per cent of the total goods revenue of £640,070, in 1931-32 it accounted for 39 per cent of a total goods revenue of £347,123".[252] The dependence on the Congolese transit traffic explained the financial difficulties that, according to official sources, were "much more serious than that imposed on the majority of British Railways in Africa during these years of trade depression".[253]

The sharp decline of the transit traffic resulted from three factors along with the general trade depression. The stoppage of investment programmes in Belgian Burundi, and the reduction of copper production from 200,000 tons to 40,000 tons had to be accepted while the policy to divert traffic to the Atlantic route aroused opposition from Tanganyika Railways.[254]

In spite of the efforts the east coast route lost the former attraction simply as the Belgian colonial authorities adopted the policy of Voyages par les voies nationales. Freight landed at the Atlantic port of Matidi received preferential status with import duty and cargo cost. This explained that the land traffic from Matadi to Usumbura, the present Bujumbura on Lake Tanganyika, was cheaper than the east coast freight through Dar es Salaam:

Route	Freight charges
Matadi to Usumbura	Francs 3,000 per ton
DSM to Usumbura	Francs 3,717 per ton
Import Duty at Usumbura	Francs 743 per ton

Source: General Manager Report, 1936, p.22.

---

[250] Acting Traffic Manager Report, 1924/25, p.25; Traffic Manager Report, 1927/28, p.106; General Manager Report, 1932, pp.5f.
[251] Imports and exports in tons through Belgian leased site at Dar es Salaam:

	1930/31	1931/32	Decrease
Imports	36,815	14,702	22,113
Exports	34,600	8,140	26,460
Total	71,415	22,842	48,573

Source: General Manager Report, 1932, p.6.
[252] General Manager Report, 1932, p.6.
[253] General Manager Report, 1932/II, p.5.
[254] General Manager Report, 1932/II, p.6.

To these factors added the devaluation of the Belgian Franc against the Pound Sterling by 40 per cent in 1934. Nevertheless, the Railways succeeded in attracting some trade from Urundi to the former main traffic artery that approximated £50,000 in 1939.[255]

With the loss of its major source of revenue the Railways had to look for alternatives. The rich farming areas of Kilimanjaro and on Lake Victoria promised profitable traffic. In both cases, however, the Railways faced competition from the Kenya railway system. Back in 1923, the Tanganyika Railways decided to sell the Kahe-Voi Railway to the Kenya and Uganda Railways [K.U.R.] for reasons of economies.[256] Henceforth, a considerable portion of traffic was directed to the K.U.R. and Mombasa. As documented reasons are not obtainable it can only be proposed to approaching this decision from regional politics and the contemporary design of regional integration under Kenyan dominance. To protect itself against this competition the Railways offered tariff rates that undercut the K.U.R. rates. In the case of bulk cargo such as maize it led to a rate of Shs.11/20 per ton as against Shs.13/50.[257] In spite of the efforts the Railways lost approximately 75 per cent of the outward traffic from Moshi while the Tanga Line handled only 70 per cent of the traffic into Moshi.[258] The redirection of traffic equalled an annual revenue loss of £10,000.[259] Even worse, the Tanganyika Railways was forced under the Report of the East African Commission to adjust its tariff rates to the K.U.R. whereby it lost further ground.[260] In consequence, two thirds of the coffee exports from Kilimanjaro was shipped to Mombasa.[261] This pattern changed with the establishment of coffee curing plants at Moshi in 1936 as before this date the only processing plants existed in Mombasa harbour.[262] However, K.U.R. reduced its entire tariff rates system as one element for export enhancement. Therefore, Tanganyika coffee exporters favoured the more lucrative alternative so that in 1939 not more than 1,800 tons or 27 per cent were handled by the Tanganyika Railways.[263] The following table documenting the direction of all trades in 1939 gives further evidence of the unequal distribution:

---

[255] General Manager Report, 1939, p.23.
[256] General Manager Report, 1923, p.1.
[257] Traffic Department, Annual Report, 1923, p.37.
[258] Acting Traffic Manager Report, 1924, p.26.
[259] General Manager Report, 1926/27, p.2.
[260] General Manager Report, 1930, p.8.
[261] General Manager Report, 1931, p.5.
[262] General Manager Report, 1936, p.20; 1937, p.22; 1938, p.22.
[263] General Manager Report, 1939, p.21.

Traffic	Total Receipts in £	Of which K.U.R.	Of which TR
To Moshi and beyond	31,730	22,062	9,668
To Kahe	578	561	17
From Moshi and beyond	12,844		4,665
From Kahe	4,126	77	4,069
Total	49,278	30,882	18,339

Source: General Manager Report, 1939, p.32.

The Tanga Line traffic portrays the pre-dominant role of Kenyan economic interests in one region. With the outbreak of the war these interests were extended to the rest of the territory as will be shown in the next chapter.

The Lake Victoria basin was another region of promising traffic potentials. The opening of the Tabora-Mwanza branch line gave the Railways access to the region that had previously relied on the Kenya railway system for transport. That the expectations did not prove must be looked after the commercial structures. Evidently, cotton formed the most important cash crop. The local peasant production was sold to ginneries run by British and Indian companies with linkages to processing plants and textile mills in Britain and India. These companies had established their position in Uganda, the major cotton producing area in East Africa. For obvious reasons these companies directed the Tanganyika cotton towards existing logistical network, that are the Kenya railways and the port facilities at Mombasa. It must be added that colonial policy guided by the model of Indirect Rule discouraged the establishment of local ginneries by the Empire Cotton Growing Corporation and the British East Africa Corporation. These companies closed their plants in 1930 after some years of operation.[264] Under the impact of the economic depression the colonial government formed a large-scale economic support scheme for peasant cotton production, the only one in Tanganyika. The scheme's success did not alter the established commercial structure as is documented by the regional trade figures for 1939:

Station/Port	Volume of Cargo in £	via Mombasa	via DSM
Bukoba	50,137	47,911	2,226
Musoma	17,889	14,922	2,967
Nungwe	6,750	5,819	931
Mwanza	48,292	19,621	28,671
Total	123,068	88,273	34,795

Source: General Manager Report, 1939, pp.29-31.

---

[264] See Maguire, Toward 'Uhuru' in Tanzania, pp.81-111; Iliffe, Modern History of Tanganyika, pp.295-6; 298-9; 316-7.

It must be added that the boat traffic on Lake Victoria played a significant role in the direction of traffic. Being beyond the scope of our analysis it suffices to outline that this traffic failed to be co-ordinated with the commercial interests of the Railways although the lake traffic was managed by the Railway Administration.

With the Congolese transit traffic under sharp contraction, the traffic in the territory's major producing regions contested by the K.U.R., and preferential tariff rates for sisal exporters the Railways commercial success depended on the economic growth of colonial Tanganyika that it could not influence. It follows that the Railways' commercial position rested on a very precarious basis. The next table summarises the tonnage and revenue earning that mirrors the dependence on the colony's economic cycle:

Year	Passengers		Goods		Revenue
	Number	Revenue	Tonnage	Revenue	
1921/22	202,480	56,631	58,559	134,013	190,644
1922/23	190,834	58,311	79,263	159,789	218,100
1923/24	234,048	65,324	89,689	164,526	229,850
1924/25	325,710	73,619	120,665	227,974	301,593
1925/26	349,237	80,922	N.a.	298,067	378,988
1926/27	416,290	102,794	164,948	347,749	450,543
1927/28	478,625	123,381	214,283	438,643	562,024
1928/29	535,404	137,458	N.a.	527,790	665,248
1929/30	538,750	147,863	N.a.	540,087	687,950
1930/31	544,980	139,436	N.a.	640,070	779,506
1931/32	351,235	104,953	N.a.	354,544	459,497
1932 (9 months)	201,985	52,587	147,586	257,567	310,154
1933	245,435	67,107	198,270	348,004	415,111
1934	221,295	63,567	219,972	397,954	461,521
1935	295,008	70,074	235,776	479,583	549,657
1936	366,117	84,883	258,480	533,428	618,311
1937	460,730	99,302	274,611	557,501	656,803
1938	499,603	99,780	233,154	443,373	543,153
1939	469,899	90,726	228,189	453,666	544,392

Annotations: Revenue in £; tonnage in metric tons;

Sources: General Manager Report,1923, p.2; 1924/5, p.3; 25/6, p.5; 26/7, p.4; 1927/8, p.44; 1933, pp.4f; 1936, p.12; 1939, pp.18-21; Chief Accountant Report, 1924/25, p.37; Tanganyika Railways, Annual Report, 1929, p.6; 1930, p.6; 1932, p.3.

Revenue mirrors the trends of the colonial economy; until 1930/1 the revenues increased by more than 25 per cent per annum. As the rest of the economy the Railways suffered from the economic depression with revenues being halved. The period of slump and stagnation lasted until 1935 when a slow recovery started. However, the return to growth did not restore the former high revenue level that had been reached in the prosperous twenties.

The export-orientation of the colonial economy and the domestic supply for Dar es Salaam conditioned the freight carried by the Railways. The related compilation gives further evidence to the above established correlation between the economic cycle and the Railway revenue:

Year	Groundnuts	Grains	Cotton	Sisal	Copper	Cassite-rite	Salt	Coffee	Railways
1922	4,601	10,643	-	-	-	-	-	-	-
1923	7,529	7,488	-	-	-	-	-	-	-
1924	7,700	9,826	2,058	10,249	4,434	135	-	-	1,559
1925	10,845	7,758	4,450	15,908	8,739	1,468	-	-	4,204
1926	6,583	14,733	9,517	32,175	16,632	1,453	-	-	-
1927	10,223	16,788	5,879	23,529	26,656	1,222	-	-	-
1928	9,224	19,678	15,226	22,029	29,997	1,039	5,700	-	-
1929	7,554	20,428	15,475	28,570	18,538	1,377	6,214	-	-
1930	17,486	16,573	6,996	34,518	33,329	956	6,063	2,805	-
1931	2,908	14,407	4,461	37,600	7,166	69	5,871	1,467	-
1932	14,687	14,940	6,583	30,655	-	956	3,880	2,121	-
1933	22,259	47,579	6,804	13,360	-	-	5,883	3,119	-
1934	12,995	52,576	8,393	17,263	-	850	6,228	2,264	-
1935	22,016	49,919	12,470	22,537	-	-	-	4,338	-
1936	21,457	23,227	17,873	52,021	-	475	8,839	4,203	-
1937	20,895	31,480	20,887	58,723	-	-	9,549	3,692	-
1938	2,783	23,118	14,746	65,008	-	-	9,501	5,722	-
1939	3,145	30,175	17,559	63,381	-	2	9,212	5,056	-

Annotations:
- Freight in metric tons.
- Cotton includes ginned cotton, unginned cotton, and cotton seed.
- Sisal includes tow and leaves.
- Railway material for construction was carried free; according to Report of Acting Traffic Manager 1924/25 "[t]he tonnage, much of which was long distance traffic, made a heavy demand on our rolling stock"; p.28.

Sources: General Manager Report, 1927/8, p.106; 1933, p.6; 1935, p.10; 1939, p.20; Tanganyika Railways, Annual Report, 1929, p.7; 1930, p.7; 1931/32, p.5; 1932, p.7.

The economic policy of balanced trades affected the volume of imports accordingly. The major imports consisted of manufactured consumer goods, petrol, cement, and related intermediate goods. Until the economic depression import traffic equalled 40,000 freight tons. In 1931, this traffic declined sharply to less than 15,000 freight tons. Recovery started after 1935 and lasted until 1937. In these years imports averaged 35,000. The last pre-war years showed a minor decrease to less than 26,000 freight tons per year.[265]

The preceding data define the 'reactive tariff policy' as the Railways' commercial position neatly depends on the macro-economic trends. The war economy, however, changed this pattern. State intervention, contingency, and the formation of the East

---

[265] General Manager Report, 1933, p.7; 1939, p.20; Tanganyika Railways, Annual Report, 1929, pp.7f; 1930, p.8; 1932, p.6.

African economic co-operation scheme announced a new colonial strategy. For these reasons, the Railways' commercial performance after 1939 should be discussed in the broader context of management policy.

The commercial restrictions forced the Railways into the search of operational adjustments to achieve sound financial results. Regarding the Trade Department, capacity utilisation and operational cost cuts appeared as instrumental for this objective.

Capacity utilisation defines the revenue earning load per train and mileage. The running of a train causes costs such as energy and work-force while infrastructure tasks: maintenance of stations and tracks and signalling had to be provided regardless of traffic. The first economic objective must be to cover this non-avoidable expenditure through carrying freight and passengers, respectively. With the economic break-even position achieved, the additional revenue contributes to profits. To achieve these objectives, the Railways had to overcome various obstacles: inflexibility, long distances, unequal distribution of traffic in spatial and seasonal terms as well as the economic cycle.

To begin with the Railways offered regular services for goods and passengers for reasons of attracting customers. This service, particularly on the Central Line, was deficitary yet necessary. Moreover, Tanganyika's economic backbone rested with agricultural exports whose performance ultimately decided imports. The crop harvest was the peak season for the Railways that met the temporary traffic increase by special trains.

This constellation explains the below-average capacity utilisation during the off-season. Because of the expanding Congolese transit traffic the empty haulage of vehicles did not appear as matter of economic concern along with the carrying of building material to the railway construction sites. However, under the economic depression the profit-earning transit traffic came to an almost complete halt what rendered measures of economies necessary. On the Central Line, capacity utilisation declined to 67 per cent for up-traffic and to 77 per cent for down-traffic in spite of a train mile reduction of 50,000 miles in the second half of 1932. Before the crisis, the average ratio amounted to 85 per cent and above.[266] The situation deteriorated even

---

[266] General Manager Report, 1932, p.9.

further with the up-traffic achieving a utilisation ratio of 61 per cent in 1933; the respective ratio for down-traffic came to 76 per cent.[267] In the following years the situation improved. Nevertheless, the Railways faced a seemingly structural barrier as the gap between up- and down-traffic could not be closed. With locomotive and vehicle maintenance centred in Dar es Salaam the Railways had to carry excess capacity to the hinterland provinces for the transport requirements. Because of the colonial economic policy of trade surplus agrarian exports were stimulated with imports being curtailed. This policy put a further financial burden on the Railways whose empty haulage increased to more than 20 per cent of the total goods carried.[268] The Railways was obliged to put priority on general economic objectives even though it might afflict with its policy of sound economic results what also extended to tariffs. Economic incentives required an attractive cost structure that limited the Railways' prospects for profit generating tariff rates. This position is given an empirical basis through the following compilations.

The revenue situation deteriorated dramatically in 1931, and remained below the average of the twenties; despite this negative trend, the non-paying activities augmented in absolute terms and with revenue earning:

Year	Revenue Earning Train Mileage (1)	Non-Revenue Earning Train Mileage (2)	(2) / (1) (3)
1922/23	540,742	199,674	36.93 %
1924/25	629,555	191,459	30.42 %
1927/28	887,593	236,236	26.62 %
1929/30	928,579	331,472	35.70 %
1931/32	694,561	355,118	51.12 %
1933	580,829	244,170	42.04 %
1934	567,451	242,078	42.66 %
1936	662,133	339,809	51.32 %
1938	563,672	309,544	54.92 %
1941	1,161,708	29,337	2.53 %
1945	1.111,280	33,313	3.00 %

Sources: Acting Chief Accountant Report, 1923, Tables XIIc, XIIIc; Chief Account Report, 1924/5, pp.44-5; 1927/28, pp.45-6; Tanganyika Railways, Annual Report, 1930, pp.45-6; 1932, Tables 23, 23(a); General Manager Report, 1934, p.8; 1938, p.14; 1942, Table J; 1947, p.122.

The preceding table suggests that traffic might have contracted. But, export performance improved as is shown next:

---

[267] General Manager Report, 1934, p.13.
[268] General Manager Report, 1936, p.27.

			Domestic Exports in £'000						
Year	Coffee	Tobacco	Millet	Rice	G'nuts	Sisal	Cotton	Copra	Total
1929	589.0	3.8	30.3	59.0	120.5	1,485.6	487.0	91.2	2,866.4
1930	397.0	3.6	8.2	73.7	186.6	1,172.3	247.4	145.0	2,233.8
1931	247.0	3.4	20.7	51.2	28.7	707.2	119.8	109.7	1,287.7
1932	463.6	1.7	14.9	62.9	182.0	698.2	183.7	62.2	1,669.2
1933	429.5	1.0	9.6	62.4	166.2	881.8	276.9	64.7	1,892.1
1934	495.2	2.2	11.0	76.6	60.1	847.6	326.6	62.2	1,881.5
1935	486.8	6.2	14.1	66.9	210.0	1,134.7	569.5	32.6	2,520.8
1936	343.0	5.9	13.1	73.5	277.2	1,873.3	640.6	38.2	3,264.8
1937	429.5	20.6	N.a	90.7	257.8	2,079.2	603.6	82.2	3,563.6
1938	385.6	24.4	N.a.	90.9	31.2	1,425.2	380.3	104.8	2,442.4
1939	466.0	27.2	N.a.	104.4	41.8	1,223.5	557.4	32.1	2,452.4

Sources: Tanganyika, Blue Book, 1924 -1939.

The figures outline the general trend of export improvement from which the Railways, the territory's major carrier, did not benefit. Eventually, the reasons have to be looked after the incorporation of the Railways in the colonial framework what will be shown in discussing the management policy.

5. Administration and Economic Policy

Tanganyika Railways was a state enterprise. This structure explains why Railway Administration reported to the colonial government whose objectives it translated into operations while observing financial solidity. Thus, entrepreneurial autonomy was strictly limited that conditioned the Railways' policy in all elements of management. It is, therefore, arguable whether 'management' is the appropriate term that should not be better substituted by 'performance'.

Management and economic policy will be approached from various sides: capital balance, development, and operations. Capital balance defines the consolidation of the Railways' financial structure; development relates to long-term investment policy and adjustment to colonial economic policy; operations identify the short-term profit and loss policy.

Management performance will be discussed under these structural, long-term, and short-term aspects.

I.

The Railways inherited debt from the take-over. Also, as a state enterprise it followed the fiscal regulations that were imposed on the Mandate territory. These factors reason the priority of the capital side.

Tanganyika Railways acquired the German property for £33,994; the capital value was assessed at £4,895,000 as at April 1, 1919;[269] the Railway Administration had to pay interest on the capital. The apparently favourable deal could not hide the actual costs of acquisition that consisted of the initial operational deficits.

Until 1922 these deficits equalled the accumulated loss of £1,393,137; in spite of cost management the next two years showed deficits at a lower level of £1,169,256.

---

[269] The High Court came to the conclusion that the market value of the Central Line amounted to £600,000 plus interest on the privately owned share to the amount of £14,000. The interest of the German Government in the railway was calculated at £580,006 which led to the net amount of £33,994 to be paid to the Custodian of Enemy Property in respect of the Central Line.

These losses were covered by free grants amounting to £408,169 in 1921 and 1922 plus repayable loans from the Imperial Exchequer over £2,385,891. Through these capital injections the Railways' financial position stabilised in the short-run, that is as long as neither interests nor repayments of principal had to be made. As will be shown below the start of these repayments collided with the outbreak of the economic depression what put the Railways into a desperate position in financial terms.

From 1921 to 1925 the operational loss amounted to £420,024 that absorbed the unused loan capital of £231,667. Due to operational profits in the coming years the initial operational deficits were fully covered in 1928.

However, the Railways was forced into capital expenditure for efficiency improvement of operations that amounted to £795,012. These expenditures were financed from an Imperial Treasury free grant of £478,158 and a British state loan of £250,000; the remaining deficit would be covered by operational profits.[270]

The construction of new branch lines and extensions required new capital. The initial construction costs for the Mwanza Line amounted to £631,000 or £3,470 per kilometre while the extension from Moshi to Arusha absorbed £316,000 or approximately £3,700 per kilometre.[271]

Until the economic depression the capital account and expenditure were as follows:

---

[270] Loans and grants amounted to £1,820,692 of which £1,019,490 was allocated to capital expenditure.
[271] This line was an economic failure. Having been built under the assumption to facilitate the settler farms' access to the railway as the cheapest means of transport the farmers continued to carry their products to nearby Moshi by road. Also, the re-opening of the Voi line which connects Moshi with the Uganda Railway contributed to the economic difficulties; its was estimated that the Uganda Railway takes about 75 per cent of the outward traffic from Moshi while the Tanganyika Railways covered approximately 70 per cent of all traffic going into Moshi; see Tanganyika Railways, Annual Report, 1925, p.26.

Expenditure 1919/20 - 1929/30 in £		Receipts 1919/20 - 1929/30 in £	
Extensions	1,213,357	Free Grants	478,158
- Central Line	893,809		
- Tanga Line	319,548	Repayable Loan	500,794
Improvements	1,845,794		
- Central Line	1,418,171	Advance from Treasury	151,457
- Tanga Line	427,623		
		Capital Expenditure	3,198,330
Others	353,395	- under Guaranteed Loan	1,906,393
		- Five Percent Repayable Exchequer Loan	1,337,101
		- Funds from Surplus Balances	45,164
	3,412,546		3,412,546
	========		========

Source: General Manager Report, 1930, Tables 1;2;4-11.

The investments led to annual interest on loans that approximated £170,000. It follows that the Railways had to make sure that these investments would improve the operational performance by at least the same amount. As long as the economic boom persisted this policy remained feasible:

Year	Gross Working Receipts in £ (1)	Gross Working Expenditure in £ (2)	Loss/ Profit in £ (1) ./. (2)
1921/22	197,260	387,821	(190,561)
1922/23	223,719	335,110	(111,391)
1923/24	238,553	331,668	(93,115)
1924/25	333,118	354,965	(21,848)
1925/26	388,167	363,843	24,324
1926/27	461,736	452,891	8,845
1927/28	581,357	480,263	101,094
1928/29	704,463	487,714	216,749
1929/30	714,183	534,847	179,336
1930/31	805,712	572,668	233,044

Sources: General Manager Report, 1923, p.2; 1924/25, p.3; 1925/26, p.2; 1926/27, p.4; 1927/28, p.34; Tanganyika Railways, Annual Report, 1929, p.6; 1930, p.6; 1932, p.3.

It must be added that no provisions for reserve capital, Renewal Fund in official terminology, are documented. This infers that future investments for obsolete machinery would have to be paid mainly from fresh capital. Thus, credits and loans would remain a constant factor in the Railways' financial structure that, in turn, would limit the prospects of line expansion and of services. It also put structural constraints on operational expenditures such as wage adjustments, permanent employment schemes and promotion. Moreover, the Railways faced repayments on principal.[272]

Under the impact of the economic depression revenue declined sharply from £805,712 to £487,743 in 1932. At the same time, the cost management led to drastic cuts: after 1931 expenditures declined by more than fifty per cent that restored the operational side's profits. However, the interest payments persisted and caused the overall loss for 1931 to 1935 in the aggregated amount of £539,344. The following table presents these findings in more detail:

Year	Gross Working Receipts in £	Gross Working Expenditure in £	Profit in £	Interest in £	Net Loss in £
1931/32	487,743	443,446	44,297	277,170	(232,873)
1932	379,228	277,668	101,560	161,816	(60,256)
1933	448,174	319,639	128,535	264,197	(109,929)
1934	492,523	331,705	160,818	293,665	(120,141)
1935	584,371	317,944	266,427	292,360	(16,145)

Annotations: 1934: extraneous receipts of £ 12,706 included; 1935: extraneous receipts of £ 9,788 included;

Sources: Tanganyika Railways, Annual Report, 1932, pp.1f; 1933, p.1; General Manager Report, 1934, p.5; 1935, p.5.

The empirical evidence suggests that the Railway Administration managed to adjust its operations to the crisis. The operational earnings secured the Railways a return on capital of 6 per cent during the crisis. The cost management shows that the percentage of expenditure to earnings improved from 66.40 for 1933 to 49.58 in 1936. In other words, the Railway Administration was extremely efficient in cost cutting.

But, these savings went into interest payments that undermined the cost saving exercise and rendered the Railways' finances even more precarious what, evidently, must lead to question the loan policy and the role of the colonial state. In addition, as the interest payments prevented the foundation of a renewal fund the Railways exploited its substance for short-term obligations. The annual debt charges are presented in the next table:

---

[272] The repayment periods of the three Guaranteed Loans commenced in 1948, 1951, and 1952. The periods covered twenty years.; General Manager Report, 1932, p.2.

Year	Capital Works in £	Revenue in £	Total in £
1926/27	60,331	-	60,331
1927/28	100,662	6,814	107,476
1928/29	108,860	6,814	115,674
1929/30	164,202	6,814	171,016
1930/31	176,737	6,814	183,551
1931/32	245,258	6,814	252,072
1932 (9 months)	157,274	4,542	161,816
1933	285,342	6,057	291,399
1934	309,940	13,979	323,919
1935	306,281	16,154	322,435

Sources: General Manager Report, 1933, p.3; 1934, p.7; 1935, p.7.

Because of the Mandate status Tanganyika failed to qualify for colonial grants and interest-free loans. Investment capital had to be raised on the London capital market under normal business conditions. This approach was justified by the legal status that did not deliver the collateral securities as happened with the colonial possessions. But, Britain failed to observe the same legal obligations in the case of profits. Profit extraction for the benefit of British industries and trading companies was unilaterally enhanced what also applied to the surplus generation of the colonial administration. In short, Britain avoided any long-term capital commitments and assessed Tanganyika for its extractable resources.

Against this background Britain insisted on interest payments. Any suspension would have led to the recomposition of the loan schemes and would have placed Britain in the obligee position. Even more, the long-term loan arrangements included a five per cent interest rate with a 20 year grace period;[273] the initial capital was fully recovered by the interest payments with principal repayments as profit bearing factor.

These reasons help to understand the economic lunacy that obliged the Railways to increased interest payments at the height of the economic depression. To cover these payments the Railways entered into liability to the colonial administration.[274]

---

[273] The interest rates varied from 4 to 5 per cent; thus, the Imperial Exchequer loan over £1,284,123 was pegged to a five per cent interest rate; the Guaranteed Loan with the maturity after 1948 required a 4.5 per cent interest rate, whereas the Guaranteed Loans with maturities after 1951 and 1952, respectively, and the Loan from Territory were linked to a 4 per cent interest rate; General Manager Report, 1939, p.13.
[274] In 1927, the Railways accounts were separated from those of the Territory. The Railways paid interest to the colonial administration on the amount of £151,416 which was the value of the floating assets held by the Railways; General Manager Report, 1933, p.18. The deficiency coverage for 1919/20 and 1920/21 were excluded from the liability accounts as were the coverage for 1921/22 to 1925/26 against the Imperial Exchequer. In the first case, repayment would be activated if the Railways form a separate entity whereas in the latter case the question of repayment was deferred until 1938; General Manager Report, 1935, p.7.

The respective arrangements equalled £153,066 in 1933;[275] £90,000 in 1934;[276] and £20,000 in 1935.[277] Eventually, the colonial power let the colony pay for the capital costs that "has been expended on opening up the Territory".[278]

After 1935, the Railways restored its profitability at a higher level. In spite of the general economic improvement the Railways potential of growth was limited for two reasons. First, the Congolese transit traffic was definitely lost as "every country is making [...] efforts to secure that its own transport requirements are met by its own transport systems".[279] Second, "it is difficult to see how [Tanganyika] can produce enough agricultural produce to make the Railway pay. It has not the rich hinterland of the Kenya and Uganda Railway with its long haul traffic untapped by competition. [...] This Railway has not even a large town inland to create traffic".[280]

The debt service rendered any development plans obsolete that might attract new revenue earning traffic. Even worse, these financial obligations frustrated the requirements for reserve fund capital:

Year	Gross Working Receipts in £	Gross Working Expenditure in £	Profit in £	Interest in £	Net Profit in £
1936	655,753	327,384	328,369	315,254	52,875
1937	691,582	337,663	353,919	312,454	83,198
1938	577,775	337,695	240,080	309,676	20,780
1939	585,172	330,175	254,997	285,092	(25,814)

Annotations: 1936-1938: net profits inclusive of all services; 1939: inclusive of extraneous receipts and expenditure of £4,395 and 114, respectively.

Sources: General Manager Report, 1936, p.9; 1937, p.11; 1938, p.11; 1939, p.11.

The annual surplus went into the reduction of liability with the colonial administration that, in turn, financed the initial stock of £50,000 for the Renewal Fund as was introduced in 1936.[281] However, after two years, the scheme was revised. Henceforth, the colonial administration will set aside a special Reserve Fund (Railways Renewal) to which it contributes annual instalments of £50,000. The Railways will finance the

---

[275] General Manager Report, 1933, p.2.
[276] General Manager Report, 1934, p.7.
[277] General Manager Report, 1935, p.7.
[278] General Manager Report, 1933, p.18.
[279] General Manager Report, 1936, p.49. The identical statement was repeated in the 39' report; General Manager Report, 1939, p.63.
[280] General Manager Report, 1933, p.6.
[281] General Manager Report, 1936, p.9.

actual renewal expenditure from this fund for which an interest rate of four per cent is charged. Under the same scheme the Railways was obliged to liquidate liability from the annual net surplus to the extent of £50,000. Any excess surplus will be added to the Reserve Fund.[282]

This scheme was inefficient as according to official estimates the total arrears of renewals amounted to at least £820,000. This estimate was based not on the contemporary value but on the costs of acquisition. Also, the estimate did not consider the German assets the replacement value of which was calculated at £4,000,000.[283]

Eventually, the Railways was seriously undercapitalised what implied that the future operational efficiency could not be secured through the existing financial structure. Undercapitalisation corresponded to the structural indebtedness. Both factors threatened any prospects of financial solidity. It must be concluded that the Railways formed an auxiliary element in the colonial design of valorisation. Why the Railways was not attributed to the pioneer role in capitalistic accumulation similar to the industrialised economies remains an open question. Apparently, the colonial power after 1919 remained in serious problems at all fronts that explains why risk-avoiding schemes substituted for long-term financial commitments. In any case, a serious financial crisis was impending. This was admitted by the Railway Administration: "The Railway and the Port Services are operated on such narrow margins that the slightest set-back financially embarrasses the Administration."[284] The outbreak of the war appeared as the unexpected windfall that solved many financial problems.

During the war years goods traffic increased from 236,512 tons to 357,359 what resulted in the revenue increase from £469,228 to £638,536. Also, passenger traffic rose from 511,869 issued tickets to 1,524,087 in 1945; the increase was mainly owed to the movements of troops and refugees.

A. Goods traffic

Year	Ton miles (thousands)	Year	Ton miles (thousands)
1933	41,371	1940	57,677
1934	43,022	1941	61,944
1935	51,656	1942	72,505
1936	58,601	1943	81,154
1937	64,473	1944	72,021
1938	44,460	1945	81,441
1939	45,238	1946	92,714

---

[282] The scheme was retrospective from 1936 for an initial period of five years; General Manager Report, 1938, p.10.
[283] General Manager Report, 1936, p.10.
[284] General Manager Report, 1939, p.10.

B. Passenger traffic

Year	Passenger miles (thousands)	Year	Passenger miles (thousands)
1939	35,267	1943	119,311
1940	36,841	1944	135,468
1941	41,070	1945	136,368
1942	72,571	1946	123,712

Source: Tanganyika Railways, Annual Report, 1946, pp.1-3.

The related revenue augmented beyond the calculated break-even point of £1 million:[285]

Year	Gross Working Receipts in £	Gross Working Expenditure in £	Share of Renewal Fund in £	Gross Profits in £	Interest Charges in £	Net Profit/ Loss in £
1938	577,775	337,695	N.a.	240,080	226,765	13,315
1939	577,553	324,794	N.a.	252,759	226,240	26,519
1940	613,889	328,581	N.a.	285,308	226,243	59,065
1941	703,202	327,804	N.a.	375,398	285,381	90,017
1942	882,109	463,868	100,000	418,241	276,482	141,759
1943	985,259	685,422	220,000	299,837	*244,000	*55,637
1944	1,025,131	754,333	237,150	270,798	211,908	58,890
1945	1,091,704	770,456	193,900	321,248	212,969	108,279

Annotation: * extrapolation
Source: Tanganyika Railways, Annual Report, 1947, p.87.

Due to these factors, the railways' financial position improved dramatically. From 1940 to 1945, the Railways accumulated net profits to the extent of £513,647 besides the reserve capital formation of £751,050. It seems that the war economy placed the Railways on a sound financial basis. But, according to the pre-war arrangements, the Railways was obliged to the reduction of liability to the colonial government.

Immediately after the war, the Railways faced various challenges. First, the colonial power introduced the idea of state-centred planning. For Tanganyika a ten-year development and welfare plan were designed with estimated costs of £19,186,000 from which over £3,5 million was reserved for road construction and improvement. Second, Tanganyika Railways had to embark on modernisation because of the run-

---

[285] According to the General Manager "[t]o place the Tanganyika Railways and Port Services in a satisfactory position the revenue from all services should be at least £1,000,000 per annum"; General Manager Report, 1932, p.6.

down locomotives and rolling stock. The acquisition of 30 locomotives and 430 wagons was imperative for cost reasons and for the increased demand by the groundnut scheme. This scheme required goods handling and traffic. In 1947 and 1948, the scheme's peak years, the railways carried more than 34,000 tons and 58,000 of cement and petrol, respectively, what mainly contributed to the railways' record profit in 1947 that was £318,493.[286] Almost £290,000 was allocated to the Renewals Fund.

Tanganyika Railways abolished any expansion schemes under the impact of the economic depression and the following debt commitments. Therefore, the railway system did not reach all prosperous areas, and, even more important, it was forced to high tariff rates. Both factors reason the spread of motor traffic competition. The post-war modernisation scheme favoured road transport whose competitiveness would be enhanced significantly. According to the report of the railways' Chief Engineer, J.R. Farquharson, road transport operated at much lower costs estimated for the usual three ton truck at 70 cents per vehicle-mile.

Regarding the modernisation of the Railways the substitution of old engines and rolling stock was necessary; but, it was doubtful whether it would contribute to substantial increases of productivity. Also, the debt obligations persisted, and both elements put the Railways in a poor situation against road traffic competition. It must be added that the boom inflicted by the Groundnuts scheme was short-lived for reasons of project design.

Finally, under war requirements the East African Federation had been put into action. The struggle of the Kenyan settler and industrial community for wider control gained full recognition after 1945. The Federation corresponded with the colonial power's design of inter-regional economic units that would render large-scale investments feasible. The Federation foreclosed the prospects of Tanganyika that became the auxiliary economy for Kenya.

For reasons of cost saving synergy the Federation also extended to infrastructure services. In the past, the Kenya and Uganda Railways had exceeded the Tanganyika Railways in profits for one simple reason. It connected the prosperous hinterland (Uganda and the Kenyan highlands) with the coast so that empty haulage was reduced that riddled the Central Line. This advantage translated into lower tariff rates

---

[286] Revenue amounted to £1,883,996 while expenditure stood at £1,252,298. Loan charges equalled £307,214.

compared to the Tanganyika Railways that lost the lucrative trade of the Kilimanjaro and Lake Victoria regions to the K.U.R.

The decision for amalgamation of the East African railway system was economically sound. However, that the Tanganyika Railways was incorporated into the K.U.R. outlines the political power play. Particularly if the potentials of the railways for economic development are considered the strengthening of the Tanganyika Railways would be the better alternative simply because the K.U.R. already operated at the optimum from the development perspective.

The colonial power had approached the railway as a vehicle of cheap transport. This approach explains the financial policy of 'credit peonage'. From the beginning, the Railways was undercapitalised what made loans vital. As these loans were linked to a strictly commercial conditionality the Railways' surplus went into debt service that blocked productivity increases. The credit policy persisted throughout the general economic situation what forced the Railways to deep cost cuts primarily for the financial obligations. For these reasons the Railways must fail to meet development objectives and to offer working conditions above the exploitation line.

II.

The Railways' economic performance resulted from the general development. Because of the absence of an efficient export-oriented industry and the lack of a strong private sector Tanganyika's future development depended on financial resources generated by the colonial power. State-centred growth conflicted with the Railways' sound financing and created the historical impasse wherein the Tanganyika Railways had to fail as the 'economic pull factor':
- Economic growth did not translate into financial solidity of the Railways for reasons of debt obligations while
- the Railways frustrated economic incentives because of low productivity and inflexible tariff rates that followed from debt service.

These factors notwithstanding, feasible studies for new lines and railway extension work started in the twenties.

The East African Commission Report of 1925 delivered the blue-print for future railway development.[287] It recommended i) the extension of the Tabora-Mwanza line to Shinyanga; ii) the extension of the Tanga Line from Moshi to Arusha; iii) the construction of the Lake Nyasa line from Ngerengere - at Km 145 of the Central Line - through the Kilombero Valley to Manda on Lake Nyasa; iv) the construction of a line from Moshi to Dodoma that would connect the colony's two railway systems; and v) the re-opening of the Voi Line connecting the Tanganyika Railways with the Uganda Railway.

From these schemes only the Tabora-Mwanza branch line (opened for traffic in 1928),[288] the Moshi-Arusha extension (completed in 1929),[289] and the Voi Line developed.

The other projected schemes, whatever highly controversial they might have been, were abandoned by the outbreak of the economic depression. The only extension work in the thirties was the Manyoni-Kinyangari Line that was commissioned immediately before the economic crisis[290] and opened for public traffic in mid-1934.[291]

Regarding the financial side the same pattern of overall finances applied to these new capital works, as well.

The Tabora-Mwanza branch line consumed £657,000 to be financed under the Guaranteed Loan arrangement. Detailed figures are not obtainable as for accounting the branch line was subsumed under the Central Line. The total value of traffic from the Lake Victoria region averaged £120,000 per annum. The bulk of traffic, c.70 per cent, was carried by the Kenya railway system that also operated the Lake shipping. Considering the estimated annual debt charges of £50,000 it is evident that this line produced serious deficits. However, if the colonial administration portrayed political prowess instead of a conciliatory attitude against Kenya the branch line would be profitable given the value of traffic.[292]

The Moshi-Arusha branch line came to final cost of £315,964 that generated loan charges of £19,494; considering depreciation, and working costs the annual cost

---

[287] For the report's recommendations see General Manager Report, 1925/26, p.5.
[288] General Manager Report, 1929, p.6.
[289] General Manager Report, 1930, p.5.
[290] General Manager Report, 1930, p.6.
[291] General Manager Report, 1937, p.27.
[292] General Manager Report, 1939, pp.29-31.

amounted to £30,600. Between 1930 and 1939, the line's accumulated earnings of £111,800 contrasted with the total cost of £306,000 that produced the cash deficit, exclusive of depreciation, of £143,200.[293] Similar to the Mwanza Line the Kenya railway system profited from this line. The export traffic from the Kilimanjaro region was directed by way of the Voi Line. It connected the Tanganyika system to the Kenya railways for reasons of attractive tariff rates and efficient port handling facilities at Mombasa. The same applied to imports. Almost two thirds of the traffic on the Moshi-Arusha line was linked to the Kenya system what explains the financial problems.

The Manyoni-Kinyangiri branch line came to final cost of £537,570 that was financed from the Guaranteed Loan maturing in 1951. The annual debt charges amounted to £31,174. To this added the rolling stock valued at £16,860 together with the financial cost. The annual capital cost amounted to £32,182 along with depreciation of £7,600. The operational cost equalled £4,971. This brings the total annual cost to c.£45,000. On the revenue side, earnings approximated £20,000 only:

YEAR	TOTAL ANNUAL COST IN £	TOTAL RECEIPTS IN £	DEFICIT IN £
1932 (6 months)	22,300	3,000	19,300
1933	43,400	4,900	38,500
1934	44,000	6,100	37,900
1935	44,600	13,000	31,600
1936	44,900	16,200	28,700
1937	44,800	19,500	25,300
1938	45,100	10,200	34,900
1939	45,100	13,100	32,000

Sources: General Manager Report, 1937, pp.26f; 1938, p.25; 1939, p.25.

By the end of 1939, the accumulated net loss amounted to £262,500. Regarding the low and even slightly decreasing traffic volume this branch line was a financial failure, let alone any development effects. This line also outlines misconceptions in development planning as the colonial state failed to enhance agrarian modernisation in the potentially rich Shinyanga region. Groundnuts remained the only cash crop whose poor harvests contributed to the financial disaster.

The preceding case studies outline how the development of new branch lines must fail either because of a strategic mistake in line construction, as was the case of the Manyoni Line, or of the underrated competition from the Kenya system. In all cases,

---

[293] General Manager Report, 1938, p.26; 1939, p.26.

the new lines had to fail for financial reasons as the colonial power was not willing to sink funds into long-term development. That the Railway Administration adopted the extension policy although the conditionalities were known must be approached from lack of autonomy, the most likely explanation, but probably also from lack of competence.

III.

Financial obligations forced the Railways into operational adjustment. Cost reductions in combination with productivity increases were constant factors in railway politics. As the activated resources mainly went into the debt service neither the material foundations nor the quality of staff improved. The ensuing depletion of substance put the Railways in a rather precarious position whereby its potential contribution towards economic and social development was sacrificed.

That the Railways reacted to the economic crisis through staff redundancies and reductions of train operations are measures any enterprise is forced to take under these circumstances. Regarding employment the Railways, however, placed the future operations on these cuts that promised higher productivity in combination with reduced staff expenditure. The following table summarises the general trend:

YEAR	PASSENGERS CARRIED	PAYING GOODS CARRIED	TRAFFIC TRAIN KILOMETRES (TTK)	STAFF
1927/28	478,625	214,283	887,593	2,881
1928/29	535,404	231,936	903,469	2,787
1930/31	554,980	318,688	1,108,242	2,887
1933	245,435	198,353	824,999	1,663
1935	295,008	235,776	905,465	1,696
1938	499,603	247,965	1,039,597	1,591
1940	511,869	236,525	1,113,807	2,382
1945	1,524,086	372,314	1,557,701	2,387

Sources: Tanganyika Railways, Annual Report, 1929, p.6; 1931, p.1; 1947, p.87; General Manager Report, 1933, p.4; 1935, p.8.

The effect of cost management is evident:
- 1927 and 1938 are almost identical with passengers and cargo carried. However, in 1938 the work was performed by a staff reduced by 44 per cent.
- In 1945 passenger traffic almost tripled while cargo traffic increased by 73 per cent (base year: 1927), the work force was 17 per cent lower than in 1927.

The next table outlines the drastic productivity increases as measured by net earnings per person:

Year	Net earnings per TTK in Shs.	Net earnings per head in £
1927/28	2/8	52.83
1928/29	5/5	84.43
1930/31	4/-	89.52
1933	4/1	107.50
1935	8/10	177.31
1938	4/6	178.55
1940	5/5	120.37
1945	4/7	197.42

Source: see preceding table

Apparently, the traffic mileage was augmented what explains the modest increases in net earnings per traffic train kilometre.

Moreover, the higher productivity was not accompanied from additional machinery investment and related improvements as between 1930 and 1939 the Railways invested c.£58,000 for this purpose. The machinery-to-capital expenditure declined from 8 per cent to 6.7 per cent. In other words, a reduced number of staff operated the same equipment for increased work loads per person. This trend, correlated to the preceding information on the extended train operation, leads to the conclusion that i) physical exploitation of staff augmented dramatically what ii) was the key factor of successful productivity adjustment.

The following table summarises the monetary effects of cost reductions; it shows where cuts took place and how it effected the overall cost structure:

Year	1929/30 in £		1939 in £		Reduction between 1928/9 and 1939	
Supervision/ Administration	113,343	(24%)	79,407	(37%)	33,936	(30%)
Work place costs (wages, tools, auxiliary material)	190,548	(41%)	118,446	(40%)	72,102	(38%)
Overhead costs	161,220	(35%)	96,170	(33%)	65,050	(40%)
Total	465,111	(100%)	294,023	(100%)	171,088	(37%)

Source: Tanganyika Railways, Annual Report, 1930, pp.47-51; General Manager Report, 1939, pp.90-5.

The empirical data portrays the extent of cuts that were substantial for labour-intensive works. At the same time, the number of staff was reduced by 24 per cent while the redundancy rate of African staff amounted to 20 per cent.[294] At first sight, these measures indicate that i) the employed staff received lower wages; ii) it operated with lesser material; and iii) cheaper African labour substituted higher-paid Indian workers. For these factors working costs per person that equalled £21.02 in 1929/30, declined to £16.33 in 1939 or by more than 22 per cent.

From a management perspective, it becomes evident that the Railways adopted the enhancement of labour-intensive works in what it was supported from cheap African labour. It also becomes evident that productivity increases followed from the reduction of the work force and the costs at the work place.

Eventually, this policy did not offer any long-term solution for improved performance and efficiency. On the contrary, it should be measured by contingency planning oriented at short-term effects that, deliberately, took the erosion of substance into account. The obvious disdain of work ethics as expressed by adequate pay, working hours, and condition at work site renders the Railways the features of a colonial enterprise.

---

[294] Tanganyika Railways, Annual Report, 1930, p.85; General Manager Report, 1939, p.139.

6. Work Place Reality

The following account tries to identify some elements in the work place reality at the Railways. Evidently foremostly African labour was exposed to discrimination. However, as with any employment situation unskilled labour was mainly effected along with harsh labour conditions, hazards, and low pay.

I.

Tanganyika Railways employed contract labour for track re-alignment, new construction works, and fuel wood cutting. The particular task was contracted by the Railway Administration to private companies[295] that, depending on the work ahead, employed sub-contractors. Due to the financial constraints of the railways and the undeveloped, non-industrialised economy labour-intensive work prevailed. The recruitment of sufficient African labour was the main task the private contractors had to perform. Finances, on the one hand, and labour intensity, on the other, condition the economic policy whose profitability rested on the sharp reduction of overhead costs that consisted of diet, housing, and general sanitary and medical facilities.[296] Because of the supply-sided labour market the contracting companies had to observe the average wage level to attract the required amount of work-force.

Moreover, because of the sub-contracting system the profit squeeze passed from the railways to the main contractor and to the small sub-contracting firms.[297] These factors explain the miserable conditions of African contract labour to what adds the hard work load. It, rightly, can be stated that railway construction work belonged to

---

[295] The Arusha extension outlines the official policy:
Before the construction of the line was given out on contract, the question was very carefully discussed whether it would not be preferable that the work should be carried out depart-mentally. It was decided however that on principle the work should be given out to contract, if possible, in order to encourage private enterprise; GMR, Statement with regard to the delay which has occurred in the Construction of the Moshi-Arusha Railway 1928, no date (TNA/S/R/ 12729).
[296] See the internal cost account analysis for the labour contract tender; Government Circular No.82 (Regulations for the care of Government employed labour), Part VI, no date (TNA/S/R/ 11523).
[297] Cf. Acting DO Singida to Provincer Central Province, Febr.5, 1931; Circular note of Acting DO Singida to Contractors at Manyoni work site, March 1, 1931; General Manager Tanganyika Railways to Chief Sec. to the Government, March 12, 1931.

the most exploitative if the physical, sanitary, and social stress of male-dominated labour camps is taken into account.

Detailed information about that element of colonial labour is limited to railway construction work: the Moshi-Arusha Extension, the Tabora to Mwanza branch line, the railway reconstruction at Kidete (Km 318 to Km 322 on Central line) and at Usinge Swamp (Km 1,033.9 to Km 1,041.9 on Central line)[298], and finally the re-alignment at Kilosa.

The extension from Moshi to Arusha was completed between 1926 and 1930 and covered 86 kilometres.[299] The Tabora-Mwanza branch line used the German-built formation that included culverts and complete bridges for the first 120 kilometres near Shinyanga. Also, the light track lifted from the Central line between Dar es Salaam and Morogoro was used so that the first section of the new line was completed in 1926.[300] The remaining section to Mwanza, approximately 180 kilometres, opened to public traffic in August 1928. The route mileage was 379 kilometres.[301]

The last major capital works affects the Manyoni-Kinyangiri branch line with a total length of 150 kilometres. It leaves the Central line at Manyoni and runs almost due north to Kinyangiri. Opened in 1932 after a two-year construction period, the line failed to meet the commercial and development objectives[302] and remained highly deficitary.[303] For this reason it was closed down after Tanganyika Railways was taken over from K.U.R..

It must be stated that information about recruiting methods and areas is not available. In those cases which for various reasons were observed by Labour Department staff it was reported that a significant number of African workers had been recruited without medical examination.[304] This practice was cost-saving and avoided

---

[298] See Survey reports in Tanganyika Railways, Annual Report, 1930, pp.16-20.
[299] Hill, Permanent Way, p.193; Tanganyika Railways, Annual Report, 1932, p.1.
[300] This explains why costs per kilometre amounted to £1,335 whereas the Shinyanga-Mwanza section was built at £3,470 per kilometre; Hill, Permanent Way, pp.208, 213.
[301] Tanganyika Railways, Annual Report, 1929, p.1.
[302] The Singida District through which the line passed was identified by colonial government as a potentially rich peasant area; it was hoped that the railway 'would effect a change in the habits of the people by encouraging them to grow crops for export and thus be in a position to improve their standards of living and increase their consumption of overseas and other goods'; Tanganyika Railways, Annual Report, 1937, p.24.
[303] The average revenue approximated £12,000 p.a. with annual operating costs of £6,000; but loan charges amounted to £32,100 p.a.; Tanganyika Railways, Annual Report, 1939, pp.24f.
[304] Labour recruitment was facilitated by the Labour Department that recruited workers for private employers and government. The Department competed with about 50 private agents. In the case of the railways, private contractors handled the 'labour question' and, on construction site, supervised these workers; cf. Labour Department, Annual Report, 1927, p.34.

additional costs for qualified workers.[305] Exactly as construction work was contracted to private companies rules of economies and profit prevailed while for the same reasons Railway Administration limited controlling to the overall criteria of budget, time, and quality.[306] The private contractors were freed from any constraints particularly concerning labour and wages.

In the wake of the labour-intensive work applied wage levels played the key role in profit generation. Moreover, construction work was segmented and contracted to so-called sub-contractors who were in charge of the respective section of construction. For them profit rates were limited because of the head contractor. Thus, pressure on wages, and general overhead costs such as nutrition, housing and health care persisted that rendered construction work its exploitative outlook.

The first case study of the Kidete realignment reports on the social conditions. Due to heavy rainfalls in 1929/30 the track that passed through the Romuma River valley was washed away. By shifting the line out of flood silts and debris-fans into the stable ground of the slopes a safe alignment was achieved whose total cost amounted to approximately £242,000 or £7,806 per kilometre. The most difficult section was the crossing of the Romuma River whose deep sediments made shore bridge foundations extremely difficult. For evident reasons, the work had to be carried out before the rainy season resumed, that is latest by November.[307]

The Railways delegated this work to a Greek contractor who built the Tabora-Mwanza line. This contractor employed 11 sub-contractors.

The reconstruction work of 31 kilometres was carried out by approximately 3,000 African labourers. Much of the labour force was composed of non-contract workers who worked off their kipende. These workers were paid from Shs.20 to 24 per month while the work force under contract earned monthly wages in the range of Shs.22 to 26.[308] The composition of the work-force was as follows:[309]

---

[305] The report of Provincer, Eastern Province to the Chief Sec. (Dec.31, 1930; Ref.114/III/90) on 'Native labour at Kilosa for railway realignment' states that " c. 1/3 of labour force is not engaged in written contract and therefore not medically examined prior to leaving their district of origin". This situation seems to be the rule rather than the exception.
[306] Different to the Public Works Department the Railways avoided "waste of labour and needless expense.[...] technical officers have been burdened with the duty of obtaining and managing large gangs of Africans in addition to their real professional work, and results have naturally been unsatisfactory"; Labour Department, Annual Report, 1927, p.34.
[307] According to Tanganyika Railways, Annual Report, 1931: Capital expenditure section, p.2.
[308] Lab.Com. to GMR, 5th Sept. 1930; Ref. 254/327 (TNA/S/R/ 11523): "Wages are higher but the great efficiency of the contractors' organisation with the very large percentage of which supervisors justifies this; the amount of work turned out per head is higher than in any other occupation in Tanganyika". According to Labour

Head Contractor:	1	Contract Workers:	1,109	Supervising staff:	46
Sub-Contractors:	11	Workers under kipende:	<u>2,215</u>	African work force:	3,324
European Assistants:	<u>34</u>				

The workers lived in twelve camps along the realignment site; each camp was supervised by one sub-contractor. The housing conditions were poor, and the sanitation deplorable. In the words of the Assistant District Officer:

"[L]atrines are inadequate and very much of a make-shift, in any case they are merely ornamental, one glance at the ground surrounding the camps will convince the most primitive of this fact. Faeces is to be seen every where".[310]

It comes to no surprise that diseases were spreading. This trend was enhanced from poor nutrition. Although the realignment required solid rock and granite cutting, blasting, and excavating[311] the food rations simply consisted of maize flour, ground nuts and beans[312] while meat and vegetables had to be provided by the workers.[313] In view of the low wages, sufficient protein contribution for the heavy work[314] could not be expected. The workers consumed large quantities of sugar cane that stabilised the blood sugar level but weakened the physical strength. In consequence, diarrhoea was wide spread and caused intestinal disorders. The weakened body became victim to other diseases such as malaria and scurvy.[315] In spite of these serious

---

Department statistics monthly wages for unskilled labour in Central Province approximated Shs.15, inclusive of staple food; Labour Department, Annual Report, 1927, p.63: Appendix IX.

[309] The number of workers varied; according to Lab. Com. to Director of Medical and Sanitary Services, 4th Dec. 1930, Ref. 254/685 (TNA/S/R/ 11523):"4,500 men collected in camps along the new construction work; these are mostly employed by subcontractors working under the supervision of the main contractor. The workers are recruited from all operators and there is a surprising mixture of tribes".
The Director Medical and Sanitary Services to Chief Sec., 16th March 1931, Ref.111/2/104 (TNA/S/R/ 11523) presented the following figures:
"January: no.of camps 27 with 5,260 workers;
End of February: "   22 "   3,890 "   ;
End of March (expected):   "   13 "   1,570 "   ;
In April workers will be further decreased and the only remaining construction to be carried out will be a bridge near <u>Kidete</u> which will necessitate c. 150 workers being employed there for an indefinite period".

[310] Assistant District Officer to D.Kapetsakos, Head-Contractor, Kidete, Nov. 18, 1930; Ref.: 64/F/36 (TNA/S/R/ 11523).

[311] For the work task see the following observation:" Depth of the cutting now under construction, it is I understand something much more formidable than the present contractors have attempted, the depth being in one place nearly 18 metres. There would seem to be an appreciable risk if dangerous falls of rocks and earth, when lower depths are reached, particularly should wet weather set in.[...] Light-hearted methods with which blasting materials are handled." Lab. Com., Morogoro to GMR, Sept.5 1930; Ref. 254/327 (TNA/S/R/ 11523).

[312] The typical daily ration as approved by colonial government consisted in 1.5 lb. of posho; ¼ lb. of beans; 1/8 lb. of groundnuts and 1/8 lb. of salt per week; see Government Circular No.82, Part VI, 1930.

[313] Even worse, towards the end of the dry season, shortage of green food with a corresponding risk of scurvy set in; Lab.Com. to GMR, 5th Sept. 1930, ref. 254/327 (TNA/S/R/ 11523).

[314] At a different construction site with identical work the Provincer, Eastern Province to the Chief Sec. (Dec.31, 1930; Ref.114/III/90) on 'Native labour at Kilosa for railway realignment' reported that Sukuma labour deserted; probably because of the cutting of rock.

[315] "Camps are threatened seriously with an outbreak of scurvy; while there have been no actual hospitals cases so far I estimate that 1o per cent of the men are definitely scurbutive while diseases akin to scurvy, and produ-

and difficult conditions, the Africans resumed their work so that accidents increased accordingly as is summarised by the following table that reports the patients treated in Kidete Camp Hospital[316]:

Month	No. of out-patients treated	No. of disease cases	No. of accidents
June 1930	185	148	37
July	311	265	46
August	369	311	58
September	481	416	65
October	602	527	75
Total	1,948	1,667	281

Source: Assistant District Officer to District Officer, Kilosa Nov.21, 1930

In other words, almost 2/3 of the African labour force suffered from sickness and required hospital treatment. To this unacceptable high ratio must be added the minor injuries and sicknesses that for various reasons were not reported.[317] The grim health condition also caused numerous deaths that for the same period amounted to 23 cases.[318] Nevertheless, the alignment work was completed in due time.[319]

The second case study refers to the Usinge Swamp construction where an almost identical situation prevailed. To prevent future track submerging the railway bank was raised along eight kilometres together with openings that allowed the swamp levels along the track to adjust themselves quicker. The work having been started in mid-31 was completed roughly six months later at a cost of £14,000.[320] The workforce consisted of 500 Africans under the control of one Italian contractor.[321] The

---

ced by similar conditions, account for an undue number of hospital entries"; Lab. Com., Morogoro, to GMR, 30.11.1927 (6/52/1008).
[316] "The inadequate grass roofed hospital at Kidete will need replacing by something far more weatherproof in view of the likelihood of increased sickness from pneumonia or bronchitis"; Lab. Comm. to Director of Medical and Sanitary Services, 4th Dec. 1930, Ref. 254/685 (TNA/S/R/ 11523).
"Medical Department has a Sub. Ass. Surgeon at Kidete who runs a temporary hospital; he also makes periodical visits to the camps; any increase in disease would render the present arrangement inadequate"; Lab. Com. to GMR, 5th Sept. 1930, ref. 254/327.
[317] It must be added that "a large number of the labourers are not in written contract. Therefore, official statistics are not reliable"; Provincer, Eastern Prov., to Chief Sec., 31st Dec. 1930; Ref.114/III/90 (TNA/S/R/ 11523). Although the case refers to the Kilosa reconstruction work it can most likely be adopted to other work sites.
[318] Preceding information based on Assistant District Officer to District Officer, Kilosa, Nov.21, 1930; confidential (TNA/S/R/ 11523).
[319] Tanganyika Railways, Annual Report, 1931, p.2.
[320] Tanganyika Railways, Annual Reports, 1931: Capital expenditure section, p.2; 1932, p.4.
[321] According to the Lab. Com., Morogoro, in his communication with the Chief Sec. (Jan.20, 1931, Ref. 52/117; TNA/S/R/ 11523) "the number of workers on the books [is] c. 1,100 but the men actually in the camps are less than this, the figures vary considerably, as some of the employees are local natives who work irregularly. A proportion of recruited contract labour is employed but this is naturally a heavy expense in view of the short contract required. Wages are high for the locality: Shs.16 to 20 with rations. Railway labour is always better paid and harder worked that that on plantations. Railway contract work, as is always the case, has had a somewhat disorganising effect on the local labour market and complaints from recruiters about the methods employed by the contractors."

workers lived in 122 grass huts with corrugated iron roofs.[322] The unhealthy climate, the harsh work, and time pressure resulting in overtime work affected the workers' health. Although sanitary conditions and nutrition were sufficient according to official examination 125 men were forced to quit their jobs for poor health and sickness during the first three months. The sickness ratio, therefore, amounted to at least 40 per cent.[323] Again, work completion on schedule prevailed over social concerns. That this approach formed the rule rather than the exception is documented by one medical survey of labour camps along the Central Line. These camps accommodated gangs of trackmen. It was observed that the sick ratio during the dry season stood at roughly 25 per cent.[324]

Information about the major construction works such as the Moshi-Arusha extension, the Tabora-Mwanza and Manyoni-Kinyingini branch lines are not obtainable nor are similar grievances reported. Works that employed up to 15,000 labourers should experience at least some form of misconduct on the employer-side, bad health conditions, and inadequate housing and sanitary facilities. It seems therefore that these works were carried out according to the objectives set out by the Railways and colonial government. Following the Annual Reports the general objectives consisted of i) budget; ii) schedule; and iii) quality. Because they were met the respective colonial institutions, apparently, did not see any cause for intervention and reporting. Also, these works seen as strategic contributions to colonial development would have been hampered by raising social issues let alone accompanying costs. It follows that the local authorities at district level were in charge of social concerns what explains the erratic reporting.

Decentralisation was in congruence with British colonial policy under Indirect Rule. Thus, the neglect by some colonial officers for social matters and the concerns by others reflects on the quality of staff.[325] It can be concluded that on the basis of the documented cases the very conservative approach prevailed that by empirical evidence contradicted the official pro-African policy. Finally, the Labour Department

---

[322] Camps consist of portable lean to galvanised iron sheds, with a few huts for married men; Lab. Com., Morogoro, in his communication with the Chief Sec. (Jan.20, 1931, Ref. 52/117; TNA/S/R/ 11523).
[323] According to Health Officer, Tabora to Director of Medical and Sanitary Services, Dar es Salaam, Febr.4, 1931; Ref. ES 1/2531 (TNA/S/R/ 11523).
[324] District Engineer's Office, Dodoma to Chief Engineer, TR DSM, 1944, no date (TNA/S/R/ 25963): "Health Situation in Km 207 Camp".
[325] Also, it cannot be ruled out that bribery of officials might have been involved; as will be shown below, withholding of wages was a common practice among the contractors and sub-contractors whose professional ethics were very low, to say the least.

Headquarters in Morogoro was closed down in 1931 for financial reasons whereby one protecting element for African workers disappeared.

Regarding wages and payments the African workers frequently were exposed to contentious harassment that reflected on colonial capitalism's uglier side. For obvious reasons, inside information about cost/profit calculation are not obtainable. However, in one case the " Engineer-in-charge of the Moshi-Arusha construction has employed labour borrowed from the contractors of the construction, Messrs. Monnas and Co. to erect his engineering camp at Nduruma. For this Monnas has been paid at the rate of Shs 2 per man-day."[326] On request of the Railways the contractor submitted his cost analysis:

Costs	IN SHS. PER MONTH	
(1) Real Current Costs		
Commencing pay	22.00	
bonus for 6 work days completed: 50 cents	2.00	
Wage increase 21/180 x 11.7% [1]	1.18	
Posho per day: 30 cents	9.00	
Free posho and pay at arrival [2]	3.10	
Subtotal		37.28
(2) Overhead Costs for 6 months		
Recruiting fees: Shs.35	5.84	
Blanket: Shs.5	0.84	
Cooking pot: Shs.3	0.50	
1 European Supervisor per 350 workers half-time [3]	0.71	
1 African Assistant, ibid. [4]		
Subtotal	0.29	8.18
(3) Costs of Calculation		
Medicines	2.00	
10% sick	1.01	
Wet days	0.34	
Subtotal		3.35
Grand Total		**48.81**

Annotations:
[1] The initial wage will rise to Shs.30 per month.
[2] On arrival the new workers are granted three days' posho and pay to build huts.
[3] The European supervisor's salary amounts to Shs.500 p.m.; he spends half of his working days for managing an African work-force of 350.
[4] The African assistant's salary amounts to Shs.200 p.m.; same division of labour as for supervisor.

Source: Monnas & Co. to Engineer-in-charge, Moshi Arusha Construction, Nduruma, Moshi May 14,1928.

All possible factors considered the contractor expected a profit rate of 18 per cent that entirely was deprived from African wage labour. Capital investment did not apply as track laying was done by manpower without machinery support. Also, Railways supplied the rails, sleepers and auxiliary tools. From an entrepreneurial perspective

---

[326] GMR to Chief Sec. 13th March 1929, Ref. GA 6/1/4263 (TNA/S/R/ 11523).

the preceding cost analysis allowed some room for profit improvement. First, medical costs could be neglected because of health facilities supplied by the Railways.

Second, major works were carried out during the dry season so that wet day cost procurements could be ruled out as were sickness costs that were deducted from the monthly payment. Therefore, calculated costs can be almost fully attributed to profits. More important for cash involved was labour related expense. Evidently, the basic salary was non-negotiable for reasons of manpower attraction. But, license to further cash cuts existed with wage increases and the labour ticket. The contractor was not bound to any legal regulations for wage increases. Also, the foremen decided the day's work performance. In numerous cases, but apparently with full knowledge of the contractor, the labour ticket was not stamped so that the respective worker did not receive any wage for his work. The 'cost-free production' augmented the contractor's profits. It is unique that wage labour was punished for sub-standard performance. In this case the worker could not appeal to any government body but had to depend on the employer's benevolence, a situation that can only be understood in the context of colonial capitalism. Not enough of that, at the end of contract final payments were withheld by the contractors. Again, the worker was in a weak position as free transport to his home area expired two weeks after contract. If he decided to look after his case he lost this allowance[327] what on average equalled at least one month wage. If reported the employer was fined[328] but the worker did not receive any additional compensation although, on average, he had to wait for up to six months for his payment.

Why did contractors not settle for a profit rate of at least 25 per cent that even by colonial standards was above average? Simply because it was tempting certainly to exploit the outcast Africans. On the other hand, the contractors must be approached from a sociological perspective. It seems that this group ranked very low in the colonial social hierarchy what explains why contracting was almost exclusively performed by ethnic minorities - Greeks, Italians, and Germans. British enterprises, revealingly, abstained from this type of activity. It can be concluded that contracting attracted pariah groups that, in turn, did not hesitate to transgress the admittedly poor

---

[327] A case that affected some African workers from the Manyoni-Kinyangiri construction was commented by the Provincer, Central Province in the following words: "Native have legs [...] So the walk home should not be an arduous undertaking"; Provincer to GMR, Dodoma, May 13, 1932; Ref.38/3/81.
[328] In accordance with Section 47 of the Master and Servants Ordinance.

ethics of colonial capitalism.[329] Eventually, colonial authorities revised the entire contracting system. By the time it became effective the economic depression had hit the colony where no railway construction was brought about for the next 14 years.[330]

The following court cases are reported by the District Commissioner for Tabora. They should help to outline the discriminating practices of some sub-contractors against African contract labour during the construction of the Singida railway. The accessible documents cover the period from October 1930 to March 1931. The majority of cases relates to the withholding of wages after the completion of contract. Only in some cases the accused were found guilty and, consequently, were sentenced:

COMPLAINANT(S)	ACCUSED	SENTENCE
3 labourers	Mr. Guelpa, Italian S-C	Shs.20/-wages to be paid plus 2/- fine
3 labourers	Mr. Singh	Withheld wages plus 5/- fine
K. Mulewa	Mr. Carayanis Greek S-C	Case withdrawn due to non-appearance of complainant
K. Mulwanji	Mr. Mannatti Italian S-C	Not guilty
K. Kimwaya	Mr. Carayanis	Amount claimed plus Shs.10/ - fine of which 8/- to the complainant
P. Nyirenda	Mr. Evdomon Greek S-C	Not guilty; balance of 9/- to be paid to complainant plus 45/- to his assistant
Labour Off. Tabora	Mr. Yakas Greek S-C-	200/- fine, or in default one month imprisonment
ditto	Mr. Natalicchio Italian S-C-	200/- fine, or in default one month imprisonment
ditto	ditto	50/- fine, or in default 15 days imprisonment

Annotation: S-C defines Sub-Contractor
Source: Provincer, Central Province, to Chief Sec., 10th March 1931; TNA/S/R/ 11523; cases compiled by District Commissioner, Tabora.

The before-listed cases suggest that the African workers received some legal protection from the colonial state. The offences, however, contradict one quintessential parameter of capitalism: payment for work properly performed. Against this background, the sentences were too mild as is evidenced when contrasted against minor offences committed by Africans.

---

[329] On the Manyoni-Kinyangiri construction sub-contractors withheld payments for almost six months to workers who had completed their contracts. Questioned by the colonial authorities (Acting District Officer Singida to Messrs Overrdick et al. Singida, Jan.31,1931; Ref. 36/2/187) they blamed the main contractor for having failed to meet his financial commitments (Acting District Officer, Singida to Lab. Com., Morogoro, Jan.30,1931; Ref. 36/2/186). Eventually, the latter proved that his payments had been carried out according to plan (Bicchieri to Resident Engineer, Manyoni, March 3, 1931). The money was wasted by the sub-contractors; Provincer, Central Province, to Chief Sec. March 10, 1931; Ref. 38/3/52 ; Lab. Com., Morogoro, to Chief Sec. March 20, 1931; Ref. 52/A/516; April 1, 1931; Ref. 254/588.
[330] Memorandum Giving Suggestions In Respect To Labour In The Event Of Future Railways Construction; enclosure to letter of Provincer, Central Province, to Chief Sec., June 27, 1932; Ref. 38/3/86.

For the unlawful entering upon a railway platform two Africans were fined to seven days of imprisonment. For the same offence one African was fined to 15 days of imprisonment. One African being found within the railways' premises "at 10.30 at night, in suspicious circumstances", was fined to 20 days of hard labour.

Furthermore, desertion from the employer was treated as a severe offence and resulted in at least one month imprisonment with hard labour.[331] Astonishingly, and probably resulting from the basic racist connotations among the Europeans, the colonial courts rejected complaints of non-entered day's work on the labour card (kipende). African workers accused of breach of contract were fined drastically to either one month imprisonment with hard labour or fines that equalled one monthly wage.

But, the same court kept a very high profile in cases of corporal punishments by employers. One Greek contractor, Mr. Semion, was fined to six months of imprisonment with hard labour for "unlawfully wounding"; also minor assaults were treated in a similar hard fashion. It becomes evident that the colonial state strictly defended its monopoly of physical power, one of its central pillars of control.

In the wake of the paternalistic approach but most likely depending on the respective labour officer's commitment inadequate food supplies, medical care, and indecent housing were treated as major offences and the accused, again, being more heavily fined as happened to withheld wages.

It can be concluded that African contract labour was treated as the most important factor of production in the various, but always labour-intensive railway construction works. The factor costs involved were approached from the rules of economies. This explains the low wages (in relation to the heavy work), the poor, and in many cases insufficient housing, nutrition and medical facilities. African labour was used for the economic objectives of valorisation that was fixed by colonial government. Only when these objectives were hampered did colonial authorities intervene on behalf of African labour.

---

[331] See the case of Butire Kawanjile and Rajabu Mohamed as reported in the communications of Provincer, Central Province, to Chief Sec., 10th March 1931; TNA/S/R/ 11523.

II.

The Railways was the largest employer in the colony. The colonial legacy made itself felt in the composition of staff. The managerial tasks were performed exclusively by Europeans. The middle ranks were filled by Indian staff that was gradually substituted by Africans after intensive training on the job. The majority, however, occupied for manual labour was split in permanent staff, paid on monthly basis, and daily workers, the latter being the largest group. Thus, railway employment almost exactly mirrors the larger social reality under colonialism.

The ethnic composition of staff shows an increase of African employees and worker both in absolute numbers and in relation to the total staff:[332]

YEAR	TOTAL STAFF (1)	AFRICAN STAFF (2)	(2)/(1) (3)
1922	6,878	6,063	88 %
1930	12,543	11,258	89 %
1935	7,668	7,065	92 %
1939	8,195	7,600	93 %
1946	10,545	9,831	93 %

Sources: Tanganyika Railways, Annual Report, 1923, p.3; 1930, p.21; 1939, p.56; 1947, p.80.

Responding to the economic cycle total employment portrays an increase of approximately 3,600 jobs while African employment increased by c.3,700. In other words, railway jobs were gradually 'Africanised'.

A closer look into the composition of the African work force shows that from 107 Africans in trained jobs in 1920/3, according to official classification, the number increased to 1,453 by 1935 and equalled 18 per cent of the African work force.[333] After

---

[332] The exact composition was as follows:

Year	(1)	(2)	(3)	Year	(1)	(2)	(3)
1922	150	665	6,063	31/32	202	561	8,751
1923	149	649	6,234	1932	174	495	7,072
1924	149	651	5,503	1933	148	428	6,496
1925	158	652	7,370	1934	138	433	6,631
1926	182	782	7,549	1935	136	467	7,065
1928	244	864	10,625	1936	137	471	6,635
29/30	256	872	9,723	1937	140	470	8,047
30/31	308	977	11,258	1938	121	483	6,636
				1939	120	475	7,600

Annotations: (1) European Staff; (2) Indian Staff; (3) African Staff.
Sources: General Manager Report, 1923, p.3; 1924/5, p.3; 1925/6, p.6; Tanganyika Railways, Annual Report, 1930, p.21; 1932, p.19; 1939, p.56.
[333] Tanganyika Railways, Annual Report, 1923, p.9; 1935, p.29.

the war, 740 Africans occupied positions that qualified for Category I of the Railway Local Service Scheme; workers falling monthly wage amounted to 5,149 while 3,942 Africans were employed under daily works schemes.[334] At first glimpse, it seems that Africans made rapid advance that, at a closer look, has to be put in the policy perspective as being pursued by the Railways.

Apparently, railway work became increasingly specialised and differentiated once modernisation was achieved. Therefore, the routinisation of work favoured workers trained on the job whereas these tasks had previously required employees with formal qualifications: According to official sources 738 jobs were filled this way between 1923 and 1935.[335] The new structure emphasised managerial activities.[336] In short, employment became more permissive for the lower ranks that replaced qualified employees whereas the higher eschalons remained strictly closed to Africans. Because the entire system shifted towards a higher level the division of competence and implementation of orders along ethnic lines was preserved.

African advances focus on the following jobs as is shown for 1935, the only inter-war year for which detailed information can be obtained. The total number of Africans in trained jobs amounted to 1,453:

Job Specification	Number	Percent. of Total Staff
Locomotive Firemen	123	100
Gangers; Inspectors etc.	376	92
Guards; Signallers; Pointsmen; Brakesmen	205	89
Artisans	462	72
Loco.Drivers; Shunters	44	70
Stationmasters; Clerks	78	42
Clerical Staff etc.	67	32
Total	1,453	18

Source: General Manager Report, 1935, p.29.

The table documents that African advances focused on manual work on locomotives that was entirely performed by Africans. Also trackmen and gangers in charge of track inspection became an African job preserve, again a time-intensive and demanding work. Signallers, guards and pointsmen operated along a specific section

---

[334] Tanganyika Railways, Annual Report, 1947, p.80.
[335] Tanganyika Railways, Annual Report, 1935, p.29.
[336] After the war, management and administration numbered 311 of which almost 2/3 had been recruited from India; Tanganyika Railways, Annual Report, 1947, p.80.

of the railway; they performed monotonous, mechanical tasks that by that time modern systems had already mechanised. Approximately 50 per cent of the qualified jobs, according to Tanganyika Railways categories, were redundant because of easy substitution from mechanical systems or productivity increase; the introduction of oil-burning locomotives, and the use of trolleys for track supervision fall under the second category.

Evidently, African advance simply followed the rule of economies, and the element of social improvement can hardly be identified. In the higher segments of clerical and administrative tasks Africans are barely represented.

If compared to the employment in the early twenties these advances appear in a different light altogether:

Job Specification	Employed in 1935	Employed in 1923	Change 1923/35
Locomotive Firemen	123	112	11
Gangers; Inspectors etc.	376	2,076	- 1,700
Guards; Signallers; Pointsmen; Brakesmen	205	56	149
Artisans	462	478	- 16
Loco.Drivers; Shunters	44	31	13
Stationmasters; Clerks	78	27	51
Clerical Staff etc.	67	36	31

Sources: General Manager Report, 1923, pp.33, 15; 1935, p.37.

Improvement had been modest precisely as Africans already occupied a strong position in the various jobs.[337] Advances, therefore, must be accrued to cost-saving replacements of Indian staff by cheaper Africans.[338] The situation with gangers and track inspectors must be incorporated in the general improvement of tracks; apparently, the entire system was re-laid and ballasting strengthened so that maintenan-

---

[337] For the employment structure on department basis see the following table:

DEPARTMENT	1923	1924	1925	1930	1932	1939
Engineering	3,811	3,293	4,172	5,943	5,439	5,229
Locomotive	1,661	1,487	1,796	2,204	1,648	1,403
Traffic [1]	403	365	442	686	505	541
Stores	151	154	157	232	86	82
Management [2]	5	4				
Accounts	32	33	34	37	35	28

Annotations: [1] since 1930, Traffic and Wharves; [2] since 1925, Management and Accounts Department.
Sources: General Manager Report, 1923, p.64; 1939, p.139; Chief Accountant Report 1923/24, p.25; 1924/25, p.47; Tanganyika Railways, Annual Report, 1930, p.85; 1932, p.74.
[338] According to official sources replacement numbered 738 jobs until 1935; General Manager Report, 1935, p.29.

ce work diminished. Also, track surveillance and maintenance were the most labour-intensive task of the Railways. Thus, this work section was restructured with the view of job cuts.[339] The introduction of the 'piece-work system' took African labourers from the staff list as they worked only for assigned tasks.

In a wider perspective, African advance seemed to be substantial. While in 1935 not more than 1,453 Africans qualified for staff employment based on monthly wages and eligibility for pensions the situation altered in the wake of the war economy. By 1946, workers on a daily-wage basis accounted for 40 per cent of the work force in sharp contrast to the thirties where more than 80 per cent fell under this category. This change is caused by some factors. Monthly labour rendered employment policy more stable as happened to casual labour. Because of increasing dissatisfaction among the African work force in Tanganyika stable employment linked to monthly wages promised reduced social cleavages. Lastly, the post-war labour market became more competitive what forced the Railways to offer secure work conditions. The measures, whatever advantageous they might have been to those who emerged from casual labour status, must be placed in a broader context. Less than 10 per cent of the African work force qualified for permanent staff positions what explicates the elitist approach underlying employment policy by the Railways. Eventually, the Railways expected the creation of an advanced social group that would identify with the employer. Elite formation started from the training schemes.

After take-over from the Germans the Railways faced problems with qualified staff particularly as limited capital funds made heavy repair works necessary. Therefore, the so-called European artisan scheme was launched. In the years 1920 to 1923 approximately 180 African artisans underwent training in mechanical engineering.[340] In addition, an apprenticeship scheme was started. Training on wood-working was carried out by the Educational Department in the afternoons after working hours. Instruction in metal-working, however, was done "by one of the European instructors on three afternoons weekly at the Workshops."[341] At Tanga, the technical school under the auspices of the Education Department was expected to meet the demands of

---

[339] By 1932, almost one quarter of the work force was laid down; also, restructuring led to the productivity increase from 1.50 worker per open kilometre to 1.44. Finally, work was carried by the 'piece-work system'; cf. Tanganyika Railways, Annual Report, 1932, p.8.
[340] General Manager Report, 1923, p.5.
[341] Chief Mechanical Engineer Report, 1923, p.25.

the Railways which for that reason did not establish separate training facilities.[342] Two years later the Telegraph School in Dar es Salaam opened where future African station masters, guards and signallers received instruction.[343]

The training system was two-stage. Apprentices underwent a formal educational course at the Government Central School, Dar es Salaam, before entering the workshops as apprentices. After completion the new staff members expected further advance by training on the job. But this advance also applied to those members who had entered the Railways without formal education. Gangers, for example, were promoted to sub-inspectors from the maintenance gangs after having served as keymen. In the Locomotive Department labourers assisting European artisans rose to skilled employees due to tuition and practice. In the Engineering Department, on the contrary, artisans were "recruited as such as the department provides no facilities for education or training".[344] In other words, employment remained very heterogeneous regarding formal qualifications what also applied to promotion.

The training scheme was restricted to a very small number of Africans. However, it did not meet the expectations.[345] According to official statements the quality of trained African staff remained unsatisfactory with the notable exception of the Railway Telegraph School as by 1930 all signalling work was performed by Africans.[346] Reasons of failure were searched for lack of discipline and adjustment of the African trainees.[347]

---

[342] Chief Mechanical Engineer Report, 1924, p.6. The quality of training at Tanga explains that in 1925 the entire guarding work on the Tanga line was performed by Africans as were eight stations on the Central Line; Acting Traffic Manager Report, 1924/5, p.26.
[343] Acting Traffic Manager Report, 1924/5, p.27.
[344] General Manager Report, 1934, p.29.
[345] Locomotive drivers could not be trained under this scheme because the Railways failed to attract any apprentices for a work that in official classification was hard, dirty, with long hours and absence from home. For this reason, locomotive drivers were recruited from the running staff such as firemen and shunters. "These men ... have commenced as cleaners and been brought up in the routine and atmosphere of the running department, have no other qualification and with few exceptions are keen and anxious to gain promotion." As a rule these drivers were illiterate who gained their qualifications by training-on-the-job. On the Central line the African driver had been relegated to the oldest engines in secondary traffic such as engineering, fuel, and construction trains. From this group the six of the most qualified drivers were selected in 1930 "for a special course of training in the working of superheated engines on regular mail, mixed trains. Each African driver was allotted to a European driver... who was responsible for his African becoming proficient to work his engine and run his trains to scheduled timing.[...] This has enabled the services of a number of Asiatic drivers to be dispensed with"; Tanganyika Railways, Annual Report, 1931, p.12.
[346] General Manager Report, 1930, pp.9f. In 1931, the school was attended by 33 Africans among which 4 qualified as Assistant Stationmasters; 1 as Guard; 6 as Signallers; while 10 were still under training. 12 Africans were dismissed or retrenched; Tanganyika Railways, Annual Report ,1931, p.6.
[347] In the words of the General Manager: "The African possesses a spirit of unrest and is affected by home sickness.[...] It must be borne in mind that it is not only technical training that is required to make good men, but a training in the general amenities of life"; General Manager Report, 1924/5, p.8.

In 1931, the training section of the technical school at Tanga was closed because it had turned out "sufficient Africans to meet the requirements of the Tanga Line for some time to come."[348]

At the height of the economic depression, the training schemes were approached from a more realistic perspective. Regarding African apprentices the lack of hostels in Dar es Salaam was found as the major reason for failure. The 14 year old boys, separated from their families, had to find cheap lodging and were left to themselves after classes. At Tabora, on the contrary, proper housing, feeding, and after-training supervision was provided; therefore, the drop-out rate was significantly lower than in Dar es Salaam. Because of financial stress all future apprentices for the Locomotive Department will be sent to Tabora while, consequently, the Dar es Salaam facilities will be closed.[349]

Less than two years later this arrangement was revised. With the Tabora workshops closed the apprentices lacked a training centre. The 25 of the 31 apprentices were sent to Dar es Salaam for further education. This time, Railway Administration avoided the previous failures as it secured adequate accommodation for the boys. This improvement notwithstanding, four apprentices were later dismissed for "bad attendance and lack of attention to duty".[350]

Nevertheless, economic crisis led to contingency planning. It was considered to reduce the indenture term from five to three years.[351] Also, the entire apprenticeship scheme was questioned but action was not taken. Meanwhile, the Telegraph Training School was closed for reasons "of economy and due to the general reduction of staff"[352] and "direct training at stations is...given to suitable African youths."[353]

After the economic depression the Railways intended to revise the formal entrance qualification for apprentices. In co-operation with the Department of Education a long range programme was discussed that covered the standard of education as well as the work-force requirements.[354] It was agreed on an educational scheme whereby the Department of Education will provide general education and the Railways the

---

[348] Tanganyika Railways, Annual Report, 1931, p.6.
[349] Tanganyika Railways, Annual Report, 1931, p.11.
[350] General Manager Report, 1934, p.15.
[351] Under the apprenticeship scheme out of 79 African artisan apprentices only 35 were taken over by the Railways; therefore, the reduction of the indenture term would save costs without affecting the level of recruitment; see General Manager Report, 1932, p.13.
[352] Tanganyika Railways, Annual Report, 1932, p.20.
[353] General Manager Report, 1934, p.29.
[354] General Manager Report, 1937, pp.54f.

vocational training.[355] Eventually, the Railways decided that for clerical posts and station works the eligible recruits must have completed Standard VIII satisfactorily.[356] The outbreak of the war led to a new situation; the apprentices were drafted to the Railway workshops where technical training continued while theoretical instruction stopped.[357] For reasons of contingency, the formal requirements for recruits were lowered so that the Locomotive Department accepted artisans and drivers with Standard VI qualification.[358]

From the available data the apprenticeship scheme after 1935 extended to less than 100 African youths:

Year	Completed	Dismissed	Admitted	Total in Training
1935	17	2	13	17
1936	2	5	6	16
1937	6	N.a.	N.a.	14

Sources: General Manager Report, 1935, p.15; 1936, p.37; 1937, p.37.

The war economy made the apprenticeship and training schemes redundant because all available staff was needed for the dramatically increased demands. Henceforth, contingency management dominated.

Placing these schemes into perspective it can be concluded that the main objective of economy prevailed over any other concern. As African workers were cheaper than Indian staff the policy of replacement would improve the Railways' financial position. Training, therefore, was strictly directed towards the economic objective. This interpretation gains further evidence once training policy and the apprenticeship schemes are considered. Professional advance was foremostly linked to individual performance and conduct while objective rules did not exist. The African worker was exposed to license as was the colonised society. In other words, the colonial authorities decided professional advance without exposing and/or discussing their rules of decision. That African labour was foremostly approached from the economic requi-

---

[355] General Manager Report, 1938, p.34; it was argued that the main objective was "to induce well educated Africans to take an interest in the type of work done in a locomotive workshop and to get them to realize that the profession of a skilled craftsman is as desirable a profession as that of a clerk". This view preserves the paternalistic view typical for colonialism that deliberately neglected the obvious: whenever possible hard work is avoided.
[356] General Manager Report, 1938, p.50.
[357] General Manager Report, 1939, pp.38f.
[358] General Manager Report, 1939, p.56.

rements of the Railways,[359] the carrier of colonialism, is evidenced from the apprenticeship scheme. Not only was the number of Africans who underwent qualification minute, absolutely and in relation to the total African work force, but also was the scheme cut back in the wake of financial constraints. It seems that this scheme survived as reminiscing factor of the liberal colonial policy in the twenties. Why did the Railways fail to invest in its future about productivity and quality that are intimately correlated to qualified staff? Simply because the Railways formed the infrastructure part of colonial valorisation.

Replacements and in-work advances made the revision of the legal position of African workers necessary. In the twenties, the few Africans in staff position fell under the Territory Local Civil Service. The majority, however, was recruited under special agreements that allowed the Railways the highest degree of flexibility and adjustment. In coping with the economic depression in the early thirties Railway Administration laid off many African workers, paid on a daily basis. Labour previously on monthly terms had the agreements cancelled and was re-employed on daily rates of pay.[360] The policy of cost cuts could be performed without additional financial obligations precisely because of the non-existent legal protection of African workers. Moreover, employment of daily paid workers could "be terminated at 24-hours' notice instead of one month".[361]

The future management of the Railways operated with the reduced work force whose performance, consequently, was linked to higher productivity.[362] Regarding employment structure, the number of African staff members increased what required modified terms of employment.

Against this background the Regulations for the Local Service were adopted in 1936.

The Railways staff was divided into four groups; i) European and Asian staff on overseas agreements; ii) Railways Local Service that included all other employees on monthly pay rates of Shs.60 and over; iii) Africans employed under Regulations

---

[359] This is exemplified by the increase of non-trained Africans in staff positions during the war years. Thus, the number of stationmasters amounted to 185; maintenance inspectors increased by approximately 75, and clerical staff by 117; cf. Report on Tanganyika Territory, 1947, Col. No.220, p.189.
[360] General Manager Report, 1931/32, p.10.
[361] General Manager Report, 1932, p.22.
[362] General Manager Report, 1932, p.22. "As the new organization, suited to new conditions, becomes complete [...] the bulk of the work of reduction is now finished".

for Railways African Service that applied to workers on monthly employment terms below Shs.60; iv) daily and hourly paid employees.[363]

The new regulations, affecting the second group only, distinguished between permanent staff with a minimum monthly salary of Shs. 60 and permanent staff with a monthly salary of Shs.55 and below.[364]

The regulations adjusted to the civil service drew a distinction along the salary level; thus, the first group was appointed on a permanent basis[365] whereas the second group qualified for a period of three years. Additional discrimination existed for pension schemes.[366] Under the war economy the employment policy had to be revised again to meet the increasing demand particularly for skilled artisans. After the depression, African artisans had been put on daily pay rates. Job insecurities in combination with low wages made the Railways unattractive. Overcoming these obstacles the Railways offered compatible wages and job security.[367] However, legal structures required the revision of the entire service scheme that included some sections of other daily workers as well.[368] In short, the war economy enhanced a modest advance for African railway workers.

In essence, workers' rights remained curtailed. The Heads of Department were empowered to dismiss an employee for misconduct and "if the Head of his Department considers such termination to be in the interests of the railway service."[369] The workers were denied any legal steps against the decision.[370] Permanent staff, on the contrary, must be informed in writing, "in order that he may have an opportunity of exculpating himself".[371]

The strictly hierarchical structure extended to other aspects such as wage increases and sickness. In the latter case, the employee needed the certificate from a Government Medical Officer on the which basis the Head of Department decided whether the sickness was caused by own fault that was treated as leave without pay.[372]

---

[363] Tanganyika Railways, Regulations for the Local Service. Dar es Salaam 1936, p.1.
[364] Tanganyika Railways, Railways Local Service, Part II. Dar es Salaam 1940, pp.1f.
[365] Tanganyika Railways, Railways Local Service, Part I, p.2.
[366] But under certain circumstances the system was extended to non-eligible workers: "Employees not otherwise eligible for any form of super-annuation may be granted a gratuity on retrenchment after 2 years service, or on retirement through infirmity of mind or body after 15 years service"; GMR Minutes, Dec.16, 1937; TNA/S/R/ 11560.
[367] GMR to Chief. Sec., March 8, 1940; Ref. 1953/2; TNA/S/R/ 23187.
[368] That referred to manual workers who were granted the access to the Railways Provident Fund; Chief Sec. to GMR, Nov.3,1942; TNA/S/R/ 31323.
[369] GMR to Chief Sec., Jan.19, 1943; Ref. 3960; TNA/S/R/ 31323.
[370] Lab. Com. to Chief Sec., Febr.9, 1943; TNA/S/R/ 31323.
[371] Local Civil Service Board, Minutes of Meeting, March 31, 1943; TNA/S/R/ 31323.
[372] Tanganyika Railways, Railways Local Service, Part II, 1940, p.3.

For permanent staff the medical examination was somewhat stricter as it required the report from the Director of Medical Services while the final decision rested with the General Manager of the Railways.[373]

Under normal conditions, permanent staff enjoyed greater job security, higher wages and pensions.[374] Other than that the African work force was held in strict control and lacked basic rights as is elucidated by the following account.[375]

- Termination of contract due to unsatisfactory work.
- Dismissal for indiscipline; one month notice.
- Dismissal for absence without leave.
- Dismissal for being a troublesome youth.
- Dismissal for drunkenness and leaving duty without permission.
- Probationer dismissed as he made little or no progress.

These cases are revealing insofar as the workers could neither appeal nor explain their position; they simply were fired. The same policy was also applied against long-term workers:

- Relieving Station Master at Makanya: dismissed after 22 years of service because of degenerating work.[376]
- Dismissal of a 53 year old because of inefficiency. The man worked for the railways for 12 years.[377]
- Watchman, 19 years' service in Loco. Department, dismissed due to old age; has not received any gratuity.[378]

Railway work was dangerous particularly for manual labourers. The policy of economy in combination with abundant and cheap African labour conditioned the poor safety regulations at work- and operation-sites. Fatal injuries were frequent and averaged 25 per year. As for these cases, Railways provided the gratuity "which would be due to him if he had been invalidated on the date of his death [...] to his family". But this regulation applied to employees who had completed "fifteen years'

---

[373] Tanganyika Railways, Railways Local Service, Part I, 1940, p.2.
[374] Tanganyika Railways, Regulations for the Local Service (Part I). Dar es Salaam 1945, p.6.
[375] GMR to Chief Sec.: Oct.15, 1928; May 26, 1931; GMR Minutes: Sept.24, 1929; Nov.7, 1930; April 15, 1935; April 28, 1936; TNA/S/R/ 11560.
[376] GMR Minutes, Nov.2, 1935; TNA/S/R/ 11560.
[377] GMR Minutes, Oct.27, 1937; TNA/S/R/ 11560.
[378] Saidi Ali to GMR, Febr.1, 1938; TNA/S/R/ 11560.

satisfactory work".[379] The families of employees who qualified for Local Services Part I, that is permanent staff members, were provided with the Railway Provident Fund.[380] Regarding injuries lower grade employees were granted a gratuity that equalled not more than one annual wage.[381] Permanent staff, however, were fully covered that included paid sick leave.[382]

The following cases reporting on employment policy will also contribute to the understanding for the hazardous work. The cases refer to fatal accidents and injuries for 1940 to 1944 for which colonial government required further information:

- Death of station clerk M.M. Asthana "by being run over by wagons attached to the DSM Wharf Shunting engine near the Export Shed".[383]
- "Death of Engineering Department coolly No. 11257 Ksiho Mtumwa of Gang No.10 by a line. Accident occurred near Urambo".[384]
- "Death of Engineering Department coolly No. 8186 Karunde Gembe near Mwanza South while carrying earth".[385]
- "Death of Asian springsmith P. Ambaram from tetanus received by a splinter of steel".[386]
- "Carriage Cleaner No. 1196 Saleh Seleman while jacking Engine No.203 in the Loco Shed at Mwanza South sustained serious injuries to the head owing to the jack shipping and sent to hospital".[387]
- "Death of E.D.Trackman No.409 Rajabu Munubi. Supposedly the man was run over and killed by the Up Water Train which passed the previous night near Shinyanga".[388]
- "Death of S.P.W.I Harrison of E.D. and a Trolley B. Salim injured by Down Engineering Train at Km 311".[389]
- "Serious injuries to the foot of Trackman Bakari whilst lifting rails near Dodoma".[390]

---

[379] Tanganyika Railways, Railways Local Service, Part II, 1940, p.4.
[380] Tanganyika Railways, Regulations for the Local Service (Part I), 1945, p.6.
[381] Tanganyika Railways, Railways Local Service, Part II, 1940, p.4.
[382] Tanganyika Railways, Regulations for the Local Service (Part I), 1945, p.5.
[383] GMR to Chief Sec., Oct.4, 1939; TNA/S/R/ 29031.
[384] GMR to Chief Sec., March 12, 1940; TNA/S/R/ 29031.
[385] GMR to Chief Sec., June 5, 1940; TNA/S/R/ 29031.
[386] GMR to Chief Sec., June 5, 1940; TNA/S/R/ 29031.
[387] GMR to Chief Sec., Aug.15, 1940; TNA/S/R/ 29031.
[388] GMR to Chief Sec., Oct.5, 1940; TNA/S/R/ 29031.
[389] GMR to Chief Sec., Oct.25, 1940; TNA/S/R/ 29031.
[390] GMR to Chief Sec., April 4, 1941; TNA/S/R/ 29031.

- "Injury to Gateman Salim Mfaume while attempting to board the Brake Van on a mounting train at the Pugu Road Level Crossing. Gateman was not on duty".[391]
- "Death of Fitter Mzee Kapufi due to an accident in the Running Shed Tanga."[392]
- "Coolly No.6073 Uma and coolly 11063 Okeya Obillo died during blasting operations at Musoma".[393]
- "Coolly No.1520 Hamisi Mohamed sustained serious injuries while handling rails in Dodoma Station Yard".[394]
- "Coolly 1296 Bakari Mabusi died when a roller hit him in the groin".[395]
- "Two Firemen who were to work 4 Down Goods train ex Morogoro to DSM were injured by hot water from a steam pipe".[396]
- "Carpenter Selemain Sabuni badly injured four fingers of the left hand".[397]
- "Carpenter Tulsi Purshotem's top middle finger was cut off by a planing machine at E. workshop DSM".[398]
- "Engineering Gangman Mrisho was killed by a fall of mast spoil whilst digging earth at Km 34".[399]
- "Porter No.5627 Hassain Juma was killed at Km 1240 through being struck by the loom at the end of the railroad section which was itself struck by the engine of a Down Special Goods Train".[400]
- "Trolley Boy (N.N.) was injured whilst he was assisting to push the S.P.W.I's trolley at Munisagara".[401]
- "An Engineering Train loaded with stone and sand crashed into the Fish Market Shed on Tanga Wharf. The Engine and leading bogie were derailed; 2 people slightly injured but one fireman, Bomani Gunda, later died of his injuries".[402]
- "Fireman Mzee Abdallah sustained injuries to his right leg at Buiko by being trapped between an engine and tender".[403]
- "Labourer Abedi Kanfami died when a river bank from which he was digging sand collapsed on him. His dependants receive Shs 300/- as compensation".[404]

---

[391] GMR to Chief Sec., April 16, 1941; TNA/S/R/ 29031.
[392] GMR to Chief Sec., May 9, 1941; TNA/S/R/ 29031.
[393] GMR to Chief Sec., May 15, 1941; TNA/S/R/ 29031.
[394] GMR to Chief Sec., June 30, 1941; TNA/S/R/ 29031.
[395] GMR to Chief Sec., Aug.13, 1941; TNA/S/R/ 29031.
[396] GMR to Chief Sec., Oct.10, 1941; TNA/S/R/ 29031.
[397] GMR to Chief Sec., May 29, 1942; TNA/S/R/ 29031.
[398] GMR to Chief Sec., July 17, 1942; TNA/S/R/ 29031.
[399] GMR to Chief Sec., Oct.10, 1942; TNA/S/R/ 29031.
[400] GMR to Chief Sec., May 18, 1943; TNA/S/R/ 29031.
[401] GMR to Chief Sec., June 7, 1943; TNA/S/R/ 29031.
[402] GMR to Chief Sec., Nov.26, 1943; TNA/S/R/ 29031.
[403] GMR to Chief Sec., March 14, 1944; TNA/S/R/ 29031.

- "Coolly Musa Adam died from tetanus caused by the fall of an iron pipe".[405]
- "Coolly Hingu Kivunzi jumped off No.2 Loco Fuel Train whilst it was in motion at Tuna. He sustained severe injuries to his right leg which was crushed by a wagon passing over it". He received no compensation payment.[406]

These accidents also reflect the harsh labour conditions; thus Railway Administration found a work day of eleven hours normal.[407]

This attitude gains further evidence from the following case study of conditions at Railway Fuelling Stations. The Labour Department complained about the working conditions. "Fuel platforms for loading stand 11 feet above ground level on a girder frame about 22 feet long and 2 feet wide. Access to the platform is by an iron stairway without handrail. Load is from 6-800 lb. In one case of my observation (and several others by reputation) the foundations have given away and the structure is supported by bush poles with an African's conception of the stresses involved".[408]

The Railways disagreed with the findings and stated that "the men are used to the job as it is generally a family affair of handing down from father to son".[409]

This position neatly outlines the disdain about security and safety that can rightly be referred to the general work conditions in general and wages in particular.

Wherever feasible, Railways wished to introduce piece work and time work.[410] The so-called payment-by-results-scheme identified the time allowance for the particular task. If the labourer finished his work under time he would gain a bonus. In case of failure the worker would receive his ordinary pay rate.[411] This scheme required the assessment of the specific work for costs and time.[412] As these issues could not be solved the Railways abandoned the scheme that "progressed no further than discussions between the District Officer and the Asiatic Artizan Chargeman; no satisfactory basis could be found on which to work at that time."[413]

---

[404] GMR to Chief Sec., April 12, 1944; TNA/S/R/ 29031.
[405] GMR to Chief Sec., May 18, 1944; TNA/S/R/ 29031.
[406] GMR to Chief Sec., July 22, 1944; TNA/S/R/ 29031.
[407] GMR to Attorney General, Dec.11, 1944; TNA/S/R/ 29031.
[408] LO, Western Province, to Lab. Com., Dar es Salaam, Sept.20, 1947; TNA/S/R/ 36721.
[409] GMR to Lab. Com., Dar es Salaam, Sept.26, 1947; TNA/S/R/ 36721.
[410] GMR to Chief Sec., June 15, 1927; Ref. L.34/6355; TNA/S/R/ 33188.
[411] GMR to Chief Sec., July 14, 1927; Ref. L.34/776; TNA/S/R/ 33188.
[412] Chief Sec. Minutes, June 22, 1927; July 21, 1927; and letter to GMR, July 28, 1927; Ref. 10698/7; TNA/S/R/ 33188..
[413] GMR to Chief Sec., Nov.1, 1929; TNA/S/R/ 33188.

Apparently, the Railways was not capable of proper work organisation and accounting; both reflected on the quality of management. It must be assumed that this scheme implied greater responsibility and accountability for the European staff along with team work. These factors would have offset i) the existing rules of a colonial enterprise whereby African workers were held responsible for mistakes and ii) would have jeopardised the easy work attitude of the European staff.

As the scheme failed the Railways eventually adjusted the pay rates to the private sector and introduced weekly pay rates.

In the early years of operation the Railways faced a competitive labour market that was ruled from private sector demand in combination with peasant resilience of joining wage labour altogether.[414] For these reasons the Railways pursued a selective pay policy particularly about casual labour.[415]

After the boom of the twenties the labour market became more settled and shifted towards the supply-side. The colonial economy never recovered from the economic depression while under the war economy the labour market was fixed by the colonial state.[416]

The following table presents a summary of wage rates; whenever possible entrance scale and maximum wage within the specific job are detailed.

---

[414] For these market structures see Chief Sec. to the Chairman of the Wages Board, March 13, 1929; Ref. 11523/13; and Lab. Com. to Chief Sec., March 19, 1929; Ref.14/49E/29; TNA/S/R/ 11523.
[415] GMR to Lab. Com., April 3, 1928; Chief Sec. to GMR, April 16, 1928; GMR to Chief Sec., Dec.19, 1928; TNA/S/R/ 11523.
[416] During the short recession of 1939/41 the traditional labour shortage disappeared. In 1942, a serious shortage developed and gave the employers a handle on colonial government that resulted in labour conscription. Colonial Office revoked conscription immediately after the war had ended; cf. Westcott,' The Impact of the Second World War on Tanganyika', p.144.

Specification/Year	1930	1935	1941	1946
I. MONTHLY PAID; PERMANENT (in Shs)				
Clerks	20 - 270	20 - 360	20 - 270	40 - 255
Assist. Tellers	40 - 60	40 - 60	40 - 70	45 - 72
Ticket Printers	20 - 130	20 - 130	20 - 130	72 - 90
Motor Car Drivers	30 - 130	30 - 118	30 - 130	30 - 140
Messengers	20 - 60	16 - 40	16 - 40	16 - 29
Sub PWI, Sub Works Inspectors, Sub Sanitary Inspectors	70 - 270	70 - 270	60 - 260	72 - 300
Draughtmen	70 - 200	70 - 130	100 - 130	72 - 170
Tracers	20 - 70	40 - 60	40 - 60	30 - 55
Gangers	40 - 130	28 - 78	28 - 82	30 - 100
Chainmen	30 - 60	28 - 48	16 - 28	16 - 35
Trackmen, Keymen, Trolleymen	16 - 30	12 - 24	12 - 24	12 - 24
Stationmasters	70 - 200	70 - 200	60 - 240	72 - 280
Signallers	50 - 170	50 - 170	60 - 192	40 - 210
Station Clerks	50 - 200	50 - 200	30 - 168	45 - 210
Guards	40 - 130	40 - 130	30 - 139	45 - 255
Pointsmen	20 - 60	20 - 60	16 - 40	16 - 29
Porters	16 - 30	16 - 30	12 - 30	12 - 29
Watchmen	20 - 45	18 - 43	16 - 57	12 - 40
Loco Drivers	100 - 200	100 - 200	107/5 - 200	100 - 210
Shunters, Firemen	70 - 130	70 - 90	60 - 100	70 - 130
Stat. Engine, Crane Drivers	20 - 100	67 - 100	60 - 100	72 - 110
Apprentice Artisans	10 - 22	10 - 22	10/80 - 41/60	20/80 - 52
II. DAILY PAID; CASUAL (in Shs)				
Headmen *	40 -. 60	0.81 - 2/18	1 - 2	1 - 5
Dredge Crane Drivers, Carpenters, Fitters	4	N.a.	N.a.	1/15 - 5
Boilermakers, Copper-, Blacksmith, Masons, Rivetters, Upholsterers, Wagon Examiners	1 - 5	1 - 5	1 - 5	1 - 5
Welders, Furnacemen	0.58 - 1.50	0.90 - 1/50	1 - 2/50	N.a.
Bellowsmen *	20 - 32	0.62 - 1/08	1	0.55 - 0.75
Head Labourers	1/50 - 2/50	1 - 4	1 - 4	1 - 4
Labourers *	16 - 30	0.45 - 1	0.40 - 0.90	0.37 - 0.95
Casual Labourers	0.60 - 1.00	0.50 - 1/10	0.90	0.90

Annotation: * put on daily pay since the economic depression.

Sources: Tanganyika, Blue Book, 1930, pp.222-3; 1935, pp.259-61; 1941, pp.221-3; 1946, pp.358-60.

The preceding table informs on interesting details that contribute towards a better understanding of the employment situation.

First, the rise of African employees to Grade I is not provided for. This simply means that African advance towards the top position within the specific job category is blocked what fosters the colonial connotations underlying employment policy.

Second, during the economic depression all African labour had been put on daily pay rates. For some trades this regulation was not revoked once recovery set in. Daily labour was regulated as follows:[417]

" [D]aily paid employment varies greatly... from day to day because of the different war works now under progress. Daily paid employment: (a) daily rates are based on monthly rates divided by 26 so that an employee who works the full working days of a month receives the same remuneration as a monthly paid employee." [Thus, minimum wage rate in Dar es Salaam and Tanga amounts to Shs.26/ p.m. or Sh.1/ per day.] (b) are not paid for public holidays. (c) leave granted 2 working days after 12 months service."

Third, the wage brackets were lifted at the top end while the average entrance level remained unaltered. The Railway Administration protected itself against wage increases which they pegged to individual work performance. Because of unorganised labour, absence of trade unions, and lack of bargaining-power this policy could be implemented at least during the inter-war years. It will be shown below that precisely miserable pay under war-inflicted inflation provoked workers' opposition.[418] The "African Pay Structure According to Joint Enquiry"[419] exemplifies the wage situation in certain jobs:

- Fuel Checker, 23/- plus rations, (2½ years in present grade, 4 years service);
- Fuel Coolly, 1o/5o plus rations (8 months in present job; 8 months with Railway);
- Headman, 14/- plus rations, (3 years in present job; 4½ years with Railways);
- Fuel Checker, 32/- no rations, (3½ years in present position; 4½ years with Railways);
- Guard, 60/- no rations, (1½ years in present grade; 2 years in service);
- Loco Driver, 84/- no rations, (3 months driving, one year shunter, 7½ years total service).

For low wages and high living costs African labour failed to join the Railway Provident Fund. For this reason colonial government intervened and proposed to bring as many as possible of the daily paid artisans on Railways Local Service, so that they

---
[417] GMR to Chief Sec., Aug.21, 1943; TNA/S/R/ 29031.
[418] It must be remembered that during the war years the cost of living for Africans increased "not less than 50 percent" according to Cost of Living Relief Committee in Labour Department, Annual Report, 1942, p.8. Wage increases, however, did not cover the rising costs and led to further material decline.
[419] GMR to Attorney General, Dec.11, 1944; TNA/S/R/ 29031.

may benefit from the Railways Provident Fund. But at the same time the legal position of the lowest grades should be improved: "railways servants [should be brought] within the scope of the Master and Native Servants. The [...] present situation: a casual labourer employed by the Township Authority may in the event of a dispute with his foreman have recourse to the Labour Officer, a casual labourer employed by the Railway has no such recourse."[420]

The reasons why casual labour had been excluded from the Masters Ordinance (1927) were outlined as follows:[421]

"[I]t was intended later on to form a Railway African Service analogous to the African Civil Service and it was apparently meant that when the Railway African Service was formed its members would be excluded from the Master and Native Servants Ordinance, but the former railway men would be included. The exclusion of all railway servants from the protection of the Labour Department thus appears to have a temporary expedient that has lasted 16 years."

The Railways, however, resisted these proposals arguing that a significant proportion of the middle ranks did not join the Provident Scheme. This position was supported from empirical evidence:[422]

"Mechanical Engineering Department:
(i) No. of African Artisans (monthly and daily paid): 440
(ii) " included above, but on daily rates: 154
(iii) " employed on daily rates of Shs 2/35 or over who cannot as yet be employed on monthly rates
    (a) medically unfit: 2
    (b) refused monthly conversion: 9
    (c) not offered yet for lack of experience: 12

Civil Engineering Department:
(i) total African artisans (monthly and daily paid): 272
(ii) included above, but on daily rates 250
(iii) men employed on daily rates of Shs 2/35 or over who cannot be employed on monthly rates because continued employment cannot be offered: 30".

The permanent members of staff were obliged to contribute to the Pension Scheme. " The Railways African Officers who are in receipt of salaries of Shs.6o/ per month and over are governed by the regulations for the R.Local Service and contribute to

---
[420] Chief Sec. to GMR, Nov.30, 1942; TNA/S/R/ 31323.
[421] Chief Sec. to GMR, Jan.16, 1943; TNA/S/R/ 31323.
[422] GMR to Chief Sec., Dec.3, 1942; Ref. 3518; TNA/S/R/ 31323.

the Railways Provident Fund and might, therefore, be classified as being on the permanent establishment for this present purpose".[423]

Regarding the lower grades the Railways pointed out:[424]
"Allowance (for joining the Pensions Fund) was not made for the fact that the average artisan is more concerned with the present than the future. All he saw was an immediate drop in earnings and the unavoidable necessity to contribute to the Provident Fund which would still further reduce his spending power."

After the war and under the impact of rising African opposition and trade unions the employment regulations were modified and adjusted to the E.A.R.H.:[425]
"Subject: Application of E.A.R.H. Staff Regulations to Railway Staff in Tanganyika. (1) ungraded African staff: all daily rated staff, except purely casual labour serving on a day to day basis, would be brought on to monthly terms at salaries which were devised for Tanganyika section staff; accumulative leave would be granted at the rate of 14 days for each 12 months of service, subject to a maximum accumulation of 56 days; casual leave would be granted at the rate of 8 days during each 12 months of service; staff would receive pay for all Gazetted Public Holidays; religious holidays would be granted, but leave taken on such occasions would be deducted from the servant's casual leave, if none were due, the leave would be without pay; servants would be eligible for 90 days sick leave on full pay and 90 days on half pay, during each "sick" year, in cases of genuine illness.

Employment and wage policy must be put in the broader context of the colonial economy. In the last pre-war years the total wage labour force approximated 245,000[426] with c.18,000 industrial workers; 15,000 employed by colonial administration; 13,300 plantation workers on sisal estates; and 2,500 in the ginning industries. The vast majority consisted of casual and seasonal labour. These figures outline the role of the Railways as the largest employer in Tanganyika. This pre-eminence would have transmitted African advance and material improvement towards the modern sector if the colonial power had had a genuine interest in these matters other than rhetoric and propaganda. As being shown above the Railways portrayed all features of a ty-

---
[423] GMR to Chief Sec., Jan.19, 1943; Ref. 3960; TNA/S/R/ 31323.
[424] GMR to Chief Sec., Dec.10, 1942; Ref. 3518/245; TNA/S/R/ 31323.
[425] GMR to Chief Sec., April 30, 1949; TNA/S/R/ 39036. The application of regulations were approved by Chief Sec. by letter from 12 June, 1949 to GMR.
[426] Tanganyika, Blue Books, 1928- 1938; Section 23; Report on Tanganyika Territory, 1938, Col.165, p.72.

pical colonial enterprise for which colonial wage labour formed an element of cost-saving and cheap production. In this attitude it did not differ from the private sector. The wage trends in key private industries as being presented in the next table support this view:

INDUSTRY/ YEAR	1935	1946
Agro-industry	12 - 80	
Construction	15 - 100	
Mining	20 - 200	
Transport	8 - 20	
Total Industry		60 - 150
Agriculture		
- skilled labour	12 - 150	30 - 150
- unskilled labour	4 - 15	15 - 45

Annotation: monthly wages in Shs.
Sources: Tanganyika, Blue Book, 1935, p.264; 1946, p.363.

Regarding wage levels private industries and Railways were almost identical. In other words, all colonial enterprises, private and state, based their policy on African wage labour whose costs were held at minimum level due to the political monopoly of the colonial power. In addition, basic rights were denied that, in turn, led to minimal overhead costs, the second pillar of profitability.

Miserable material reproduction, denial of basic rights at the work place, and hazardous work conditioned the attitudes of African workers whose early apathy changed into social resilience against work conditions. At a later stage, this change of attitude contributed to the political opposition against the colonial regime as such.

7. The Rise of Organised Protest

Social movements responded to colonial rule whose economics and politics gave the inter-war period its distinct outlook. On the one hand, colonial capitalism remained rudimentary and frail what, on the other, founded the economic strategy of formal subsumption, that is the appropriation of peasant surplus for capitalist valorisation. This strategy followed from Indirect Rule, the combination of social containment and subtle mechanisms of exploitation. With local authorities restored colonial government expected the working of a political buffer that would shield colonial rule.[427]

However, land alienation and intervention in production led to peasant resistance. Whatever weak colonial capitalism might have been it depended on wage labour whose organisation and material compensation observed these weak foundations. In other words, workers protested against the miserable work conditions. Opposition from the social strata that were directly and indirectly involved portrays the typical constellation of colonialism in Africa. That the rise of social resistance to anti-colonial opposition took more than twenty years should be approached from Indirect Rule. Exactly because of its permissiveness Indirect Rule shifted protest and resistance towards the social level. Long-term compromise was ruled out because of the vested interests underlying capitalism and colonial rule. Thus, conflicts shifted towards political issues that found colonialism in a non-compromising situation. Exactly here, the weakness of colonialism made itself felt: it lacked repressive capacity and was incapable of co-operation. This constellation cast post-war politics in Tanganyika into its specific mould that might be defined as 'the period of agony'.

I.

Tanganyika under British rule remained one of the most backward economies in Africa. Backwardness defines the two-fold constraints to which the territory was ex-

---

[427] J.D. Graham, 'Indirect Rule: The Establishment of 'Chiefs' and 'Tribes' in Cameron's Tanganyika', in *Tanzania Notes and Records*, 27/28, 1976, pp.1-10.

posed. The capitalist sector, enclosed in exportation of agrarian raw materials, combined a sphere of circulation or exchange wherein the collection of cash predominated capital accumulation. This constellation profoundly effected the social structure in general and the role of wage labour in particular.

In the wake of the 1906 reforms German colonialism launched some initiatives for capitalistic valorisation. However, the features of military and geo-political predominance were preserved. They rendered the transport infrastructure the pivotal role both in regard of military designs and revenue collection. When Great Britain took over in 1920, the Tanganyika Mandate complied with the German legacy.

The inter-war period experienced stagnation only to be modestly improved under the post-war development planning. Hence, it can rightly be assumed that the Tanganyika economy remained highly undeveloped in the capitalist sense with the sisal plantations as the economic key sector. Reproduction of the colonial state, therefore, rested with the export performance of sisal that, in turn, effected the composition of the African labour force:

i) Sisal production hardly allowed for mechanisation due to the particularities of cutting; Furtheron, nursing of seedlings and the preparation of fallow lands demanded manpower. For these reasons, sisal remained highly labour-intensive.[428]

ii) Due to its export orientation sisal remained highly vulnerable against world market fluctuations resulting from changes at the industrial side. The plantation capital protected itself against this trend by increased flexibility.[429]

The mixed labour system combined migrant labour, *manamba*, with squatting; in addition, local labour was recruited for seasonal peaks. Economics help to understand that plantation labour, roughly two thirds of the entire colonial labour force, did not play a socio-political role according to its numerical strength.[430]

Because of economic stagnation, on the one pole, and the reliance on plantation exports, on the other, the auxiliary infrastructure was adjusted to the improvement of exports. This objective effected the labour policy of the Tanganyika Railways. It re-

---

[428] Moffett, Hill, Tanganyika, pp.433ff.
[429] For strategic planning adopted by major plantation companies see E. Hitchcock, 'The East African Sisal Industry', in *Rhodesia and East Africa*, 1958, p.397; and K.M. Stahl, *The Metropolitan Organization of British Colonial Trade. Four Regional Studies*. London, 1951, p.180.
[430] Kapepwa Tambila, 'A Plantation Labour Magnet: The Tanga Case', in Walter Rodney, K. Tambila, L. Sago, *Migrant Labour in Tanzania during the Colonial Period. Case Studies of Recruitment and Conditions of Labour in the Sisal Industry*. Hamburg, 1983, p.35.

lied on unskilled and therefore cheap African labour; for reasons of economies contract labour was preferred what improved the flexibility of employment. The predominance of unskilled and contract workers almost precluded any form of social coherence and identification among the workers.[431] Thus, the largest employer in the colony portrayed similar features to the plantation sector.

It follows that the formation of an African working class was reduced to economic niches with hardly any impact on the vast majority, at least for the period under discussion. The undeveloped capitalist sector corresponds with the pre-dominance of peasant production excepting colonial capitalism. The peasantry's set of social and emotional values was moulded by family and kinship as the most immediate vectors of reference; the related socio-political hierarchy was outside the capitalistic modernity. This also extended to temporary labourers in the capitalist sector, migrant or contract. For them the voyage into modernity was limited while the ultimate return to family and clan remained beyond doubt what conditioned the sauce-emotional orientation.[432]

Peasant opposition emerged from land alienation and intervention by the colonial state in production. The first factor attacks the vital foundations of peasant societies whereas the second portrays their complex cultural composition. The non-existent division between economics and politics gave peasant societies their distinct feature and explains the unpredictable and patently hostile attitude against the colonial state and its local surrogates. With the wise view of hindsight, it can be assumed that colonial rule in the Tanganyika country-side was far from stable, most likely not even consolidated. In the inter-war years the peasantry directed energies against the local focus.[433] Irrespective of the probable spread of peasant discontent the various local movements did not join in a territory-wide opposition precisely as colonialism appeared in a very concrete form in the rural arena. The Native Authorities, and not colonial administration in Dar es Salaam attracted and absorbed dispute.[434] The resulting

---

[431] In a broader view Issa G. Shivji, *Law, State and the Working Class in Tanzania c.1920-1964*. London, 1986, p.115, states that "colonial and neo-colonial industrialization had a two-fold negative impact on the development of the proletariat. Although it created a proletariat, the proletariat so created was small in size with a large proportion of unskilled workers".

[432] Collection of bride-wealth was one factor for labour migration, and rendered wage labour its temporary outlook that hampered solidarity among workers; cf. Thomas Hodgkın, *Nationalism in Colonial Africa*. London, 1956, p.118.

[433] What Gavin Williams,'Taking the Part of the Peasants: Rural Development in Nigeria and Tanzania', in Peter Gutkind and I. Wallerstein (ed.), *The Political Economy of Contemporary Africa*. Beverly Hills, 1976, p.133, aptly summarises: "Resistance to agricultural regulations was the major source of nationalist protest [...] discredited the authority of local chiefs, agricultural officers...".

[434] For the following see Iliffe, Modern History of Tanganyika, pp.405-17; Robert Bates, *Essays on the Political Economy of Rural Africa*. Cambridge, 1982, pp.635ff; and Shivji, Law, State, and the Working Class, pp.97f.

vortex stabilised colonial rule. But, economic stagnation was questioned after the second world war for reasons of Britain's economic crisis. The quest for belated valorisation led to primary accumulation that recomposed the former equilibrium between colonisers and colonised, and, eventually, contributed to the formation of anti-colonial nationalism. The legacy of the Swahili civilisation appeared as one important binding element that for reasons of nationalist ideology is omitted in official accounts.[435] It seems obvious that cultural ties as expressed in language, a specific form of Islam and cultural exchange deserve closer attention. Most notably, the existence of a universal language: Kiswahili facilitated territory-wide communication while the 19th century long-distance trade had established a formal network of exchanges as being evidenced by towns, trading posts and trade routes. Finally, Islam became the social force of resistance against missionary zeal.

The foundation of the Tanganyika African Association, TAA, combines these elements to an early social movement. TAA primarily reflected the attitudes of the western-educated African minority that, at the same time, engaged in proto-trade union activities. It seems that the formation of opposition started at the top of the social hierarchy.[436] This, however, is significant for various reasons.

First, it outlines the material position under colonialism. The social strata whose reproduction depended on wage labour relations protested against material misery. It must be remembered that the wage and salary cut during the economic depression were not revoked. Moreover, the war economy led to rising inflation so that material reproduction could no longer be met by wage incomes. Precisely at this point, workers' rebellion started that for reasons explained below rapidly changed into organised protest and strikes.

Second, it shows that the most advanced or co-opted segments of the colonised society identified their future not within but against the colonial social matrix.

Third, the absence of resistance by manual workers and casual labourers in the twenties and thirties portray the enormous difficulties for organisation and social identification at the work place and beyond. To this add the heterogeneous social orientation as long as the return to the peasant roots remained open. In other words, for the majority of the colony's manpower wage labour was looked at as temporary.

---

[435] John Lonsdale's observation ('Some Origins of Nationalism in Tanzania', in Lionel Cliffe and John S. Saul (ed.), *Socialism in Tanzania. An Interdisciplinary Reader. Vol.1 Politics*. Nairobi, 1973, pp.25-8) has revealingly met little resonance.
[436] Iliffe, Modern History of Tanganyika, p.289; Bates, Political Economy of Rural Africa, p.636; M.H.Y. Kaniki (ed.), *Tanzania under Colonial Rule*. London, 1980, p.361.

Against this background, the early foundations of social opposition should be understood as the search of an adequate response against colonial rule. The Swahili civilisation played the important role of focus and ferment in post-war nationalism.[437]

II.

The exploitative character of colonial capitalism in the economic terrain together with colonial racism in all walks of daily life founded protest and the preparedness for conflict. Both formed the conceptional yardstick for the identification of social coherence and identity. This view stems from the harsh economic reality to which colonised Africans were exposed. To this add the uncompromising colonial rule whose survival made necessary the denial of individual rights together with an arbitrary system of punishment. Eventually, colonialism was the rule by collective *angst*.

Efforts towards adjustment were short-lived for the same reasons - a system based on confrontation could only be overcome by the same confrontational approach by the oppressed. In this sense, any social coherence and identity become politised *per se*.

Against this background, Tanganyika in the twenties and thirties was socially undeveloped, as well. The forms of political protest remained embryonic, if at all. It is argued that the formation of social organisations cast the platform from where the powerful anti-colonial actions of the forties were launched.

The origins of mass movements in the forties primarily result from developing capitalism. The increasing demand for manpower and the emerging proletarisation of wage labour accompanied a colonial state that preserved its confrontational approach. Instead of adjustment the administration pursued its social policy of racist disdain so that the establishment of basic rights at the workplace lay with the workers themselves.[438] The early success immediately exposed the weakness of the colonial state whose power was more symbolic than real. In a very short time, the social movement challenged the entire colonial system far beyond the workplace.

---

[437] According to T.O. Ranger,'The movement of ideas, 1850-1939', in I.N. Kimambo and A.J. Temu (ed.), *A History of Tanzania*. Nairobi, 1979, p.186, proto-nationalist positions were promulgated on Zanzibar from where they spread to the mainland. Ranger explains this pattern by the cultural ties that bind the island with Arabia. Dissemination was probably facilitated by the migrant labour system; cf. Norman R. Bennett, *A History of the Arab State of Zanzibar*. London, 1978, pp.218-20.
[438] Tanganyika enacted its Trade Union Ordinance in 1932 at the behest of the Secretary of State; the ordinance intended to guide workers' organisation along proper channels that translated into the strict control over workers' organisations which, consequently, were denied any autonomy; cf. Shivji, Law, State, and the Working Class, p.157.

Against this background the nationalist movement has its origins in the emerging working class of the forties who had to form its own social identity without any reliance on former experiences.

To place the situation at the Tanganyika Railways into the historic perspective a brief account of the social events during the period under discussion seems appropriate. This account will help the understanding why the Railways, the largest employer, did not play the decisive role at least in the early stage.

The strikes of the Tanga and Dar es Salaam dockworkers after 1937 opened the period of workers' protest and organisation. Why protest started here requires a brief glance at the respective social and economic environs.

Labour demands of the sisal plantations, the importance of sisal for the colonial economy and plantation capital resulted in the early proletarisation of the peasantry in Tanga Province, the centre of sisal production. Particularly the thirties must be regarded as the watershed of social processes. The world economic slump forced plantation capital into labour cost reductions to meet declining market prices. By this step the Tanganyika producers gained the strategic advantage over their major competitors along with unique soil and climactic conditions. The Mandate territory emerged from the slump as the leading sisal producer. However, low wages had to be preserved what was supported by migrant labour and squatting.[439] The articulation with pre-capitalist modes of production favoured the militaristic organisation of labour processes inside the plantations. On the other hand, the physical shipment of the plantation crop became an auxiliary, yet strategic task. Sisal was mainly shipped through Tanga harbour as the majority of the of the plantations was located in Tanga Province.

Imports, however, reached Tanganyika through Dar es Salaam harbour, the administrative centre and head of the railway system. Tanganyika's rise to the leading world market producer of sisal attracted British merchant and banking capital that exercised a subtle influence over production through credits and a tight control over the crop's physical handling.[440] The second element resulted in the formation of a permanent dockwork proletariat. Furthermore, because of Tanga's open anchorage

---

[439] According to Tambila, 'Plantation Labour Magnet', p.35, wages that had been cut during the economic depression were frozen until 1951.
[440] Stahl, The Metropolitan Organization of British Colonial Trade.

skilled labour was needed for the lighter-to-ship cargo handling. Labour shortage and skill strengthened the dockworkers' position which merchant capital frequently tried to break through the hiring of unskilled labour. The ensuing conflicts culminated in the strikes of the late thirties and early forties wherein Tanga differed from the rest of the colony. Due to these circumstances Tanga remained unique[441] what, in turn, helps to understand that strikes and dockworkers' resistance only gradually disseminated to the other centres of colonial capitalism.

Regarding Dar es Salaam, its port remained less important than Tanga. Moreover, the absence of industries explains the formation of a temporary and migrating labour force in the port:[442]

Serving as railway head from where mainly imports were distributed to the central and northern provinces Dar es Salaam remained inferior to Tanga; the backwardness of colonial capitalism outside the Tanga focus renders imports erratic and limited in regard of volume. This constellation explains that the port for reasons of efficiency and profitability relied on a temporary work force.

The socio-economic conditions of Dar es Salaam favoured migrant labour from the surrounding districts because of the lack of industries. Hence, the social pressure that cast Tanga in its proletarian mould did not exist in the colony's administrative centre. Also, permanent employment mainly occurred in the bottom ranks of the colonial civil service and domestic services. The latter deserves special attention as it experienced the first, however short-lived, trade union organisation in the thirties - an area that still needs research.

Change began immediately after 1945 in the wake of enforced valorisation through the development schemes. The colonial power launched a large-scale investment campaign that intended to turn Tanganyika into a major producer of agrarian raw materials. Consequently, Dar es Salaam expanded in administration and light industries while the new wave of investments boosted foreign trades. The latter caused the expansion of harbour facilities and the re-composition of port labour. Because of the development design foreign trades through Dar es Salaam lost their former erratic outlook and demanded a permanent labour force with casual labour deployed in

---

[441] To this must be added land scarcity in Tanga District; the workers depended on wage labour as the only means of material reproduction.
[442] For the following see John Iliffe, 'The Creation of Group Consciousness Among the Dockworkers of Dar es Salaam 1929-50', in Richard Sandbrook and Robin Cohen (ed.), *The Development of an African Working Class. Studies in Class Formation and Action.* London, 1975, p.51.

peak periods. The ensuing re-composition of what previously had been a homogenous labour force provoked resistance and opposition. The formation of a permanent labour force created new conflicts simply because of wage levels, labour conditions and social security. Moreover, casual workers being turned redundant resisted this development. Both elements contributed to the waves of strikes in the late forties. In spite of the formal division in permanent and casual labour both groups portrayed a degree of unity. On the one hand, permanent employment was accompanied by low pay what required the search of second jobs. On the other, casual labour having enjoyed that privilege was denied this flexibility due to the registration pool system.[443] To this added the rise of anti-colonialism that put the workers' protest into a wider perspective of political resistance against the oppressive colonial regime.

The years between 1937 and 1947 might be regarded as the formative period for working class identity. The '37 strike of the Tanga port workers opened the venue into organised opposition. It gathered momentum during the war years, culminated in the general strike of 1947, and established organised labour as major player in Tanganyika politics.

The quest for material improvement and job security dominated workers' attitude. The Tanga strike documented this dissatisfaction at a larger scale.[444] Also, for the first time, workers presented their case as one body. In this respect it was a success with long-term effects for the following reason. Colonial capitalism had prohibited the formation of organised labour; it also adopted the system of casual labour. The bargaining-power of wage labour was limited to the individual case what explains that wage cuts during the economic depression and wage freezes after economic recovery were applied without (recorded) opposition. The supply-side dominated labour market ended after the '37 strike, the increased demand for labour under the war

---

[443] LO, DSM, to Lab. Com., June 1940; TNA 61/14/22/I/2: "Port work is essentially spasmodic [...] and in lean times the casual dock labourer is forced to get what credit he can or to avail himself of the services of the many Indian pawn-brokers".
[444] According to the official findings; Tanganyika, *Report of the Commission Appointed to Enquire into the Disturbances which occurred in the Port of Tanga during the month of August 1939.* Dar es Salaam: Government Printer, 1939, pp.22-5.

economy, and the wave of workers' actions in the coming years. Colonial capitalism was forced to adjust to organised labour and increasing bargaining- power.[445]

The first reported case of railway workers' protest in 1941 portrays the demands and the reaction by the colonial authorities and herewith paints the picture of social reality.

III.

On 18 December, 1941, African workers of the Chief Mechanical Engineering Department at Dar es Salaam "placed grievances before the Chief Mechanical Engineer. Workers refused to return to work unless a promise was made to bring their grievances to higher authority. [One day later, the District Commissioner interviewed the workers who] returned to work after giving an undertaking [by DC] that Government would make a pronouncement in a few days' time to what could be done to alleviate their complaints."[446] The workers on strike numbered approximately 500[447] and "consisted almost entirely of the more highly paid grades, even those in the incremental scales, and that the unskilled employees were almost entirely underrepresented".[448]

The workers complained that " rates of pay for labour are static and that in skilled and semi-skilled jobs the maximum wages are too low; cost of living has risen but wages have not. Labour Officers have ceaselessly remarked on the profiteering in DSM for the past four months and it is recommended that immediate steps be taken to enquire into the position and rectify it. The minimum wage pre-war was assessed at 29/04 p.m.. [F]ull pay on leave is not granted; full pay whilst sick in hospital is demanded; travelling allowance on transfer is requested."[449]

Submitting his report the District Commissioner added that "[n]atives are feckless and quite apart from this fact the majority of them are paid less than a living wage and have no cash reserves; a sudden transfer can easily seriously embarrass a fa-

---

[445] It is indicative that Minimum Wage legislation was enacted in 1939. Colonial government believed that wages should be fixed and regulated without state interference; cf. Shivji, Law, State, and the Working Class, p.133.
[446] District Commissioner to Provincer, Eastern Province, Dec. 19, 1941; TNA/S/R/ 30271.
[447] Minutes of a Meeting held at Government House at 10 am on Tuesday, 6th January; TNA/S/R/ 30271.
[448] LO, DSM, to Provincer, Eastern Province, Dec. 19, 1941; TNA/S/R/ 30271.
[449] District Commissioner to Provincer, Eastern Province, Dec. 19, 1941; TNA/S/R/ 30271.

mily and leave it destitute until the next pay day. The native labour of the Engineering Department is unanimous in its dissatisfaction which will probably spread".[450]

Apparently, the workers complained the insufficient pay that was too low to cover the most immediate costs of material reproduction. Colonial authorities aware of the serious situation[451] saved time and gained control of the workers who accepted to be represented by the District Officer.[452]

That colonial government immediately took over from the General Manager of the Railways whose approach was rejected[453] was illustrative of the tensions. Also, colonial government approached the Labour Advisory Board to examine the working conditions of the complaining workers.[454]

Colonial government was fully aware of the miserable material conditions of African wage labour in Dar es Salaam as is evidenced from the Report by the Labour Officer that had been compiled in September 1941. This report's findings were:
"(1) Average minimum wage rates and cost of living.
Prior to war the cost of living in DSM was very high and bore no relation to wage rates. In September 1939 the minimum was Shs 29/04 p.m. for a man and his wife without any family, exclusive of clothing. [casual Government employees, registered port labour and a very few business firms are exceptions] No corresponding increases in wages have been made by employers to meet the rise in the cost of living. The average wage of an unskilled employee working in the rice mills is Shs 12/- to 15/- p.m. for a normal 10 hour's day. Some are receiving as little as Shs 8/- to 10/- for 30 tasks and taking an average month of 25 days worked per month Shs 10/ to 12/50 can be accepted as the average actual amount of wages earned by the native in the calendar month. Moreover, except for some natives working on the night shifts no rations are issued. Casual labour is usually paid at a rate varying from 33 cents to 60 cents per day.

---

[450] District Commissioner to Provincer, Eastern Province, Dec. 19, 1941; TNA/S/R/ 30271.
[451] An official survey in 1939 reckoned that the total African adult male labour force in Dar es Salaam was approximately 6,000 of which c.25 per cent were unemployed; the majority of the employed earned less than Shs.15 per month. The social conditions were equally dreadful. Some 20,000 to 25,000 Africans were crowded into approximately 3,200 houses; A.H.Pike, 'Report on Native Affairs in Dar es Salaam Township', June 5, 1939; TNA 61/207/2/220.
[452] Minutes of a Meeting held at Government House at 10 am on Tuesday, 6th January; TNA/S/R/ 30271.
[453] The interpretation that "labour troubles were mainly due to misunderstandings of conditions of service and mismanagement of subordinate staff by the technical staff" was non-convincing as was the proposal of "appointment of a Welfare Officer ... (a) sympathetic understanding of the African ... (b) he should realise that native advancement can only come by work and devotion to duty. His [Welfare Officer] duties in the first instance should be to act as go-between in the question of African requests and the Chief Mechanical Engineer and to support the Chief Mech. in the maintenance of essential services"; GMR to Railway Advisory Council, Memorandum No.75, Dec.29, 1941; TNA/S/R/ 30271.
[454] GMR to Lab. Com., Jan.7, 1941; TNA/S/R/ 30271.

(2) Whilst the cost of living has increased considerably wages remain the same as before the war and are more than ever sub-marginal. It is a common sight for natives to be seen sleeping out at night in public places and buildings or on the verandas of private houses simply because they are unable to pay for a night's lodging.

(3) Government increased the pay of all its casual employees in DSM to 80 cents a day last October, but hardly any commercial employer has followed suit. It therefore becomes imperative to consider the introduction of a minimum wage.

The present system of price control is ineffective. Native produce is controlled [...]; clothes, piece goods, iron ware, etc. are uncontrolled and the result is that the cost of the latter has soared sharply and unnecessarily. The wholesale and retail prices of foodstuffs are controlled by orders issued under the Defence Regulations; in practice it has been found that retailers are selling foodstuffs at prices in excess of the figures fixed by Government. The real culprits are the wholesale merchants who are breaking the law deliberately and systematically. Transaction between wholesalers and retailers are in cash, but the wholesaler will only give the retailer a cash receipt for the amount shown in the controlled price list. He demands at the same time an additional payment in cash from the retailer which is nowhere recorded."[455]

Against this background the Provincial Officer specified the report's major findings in a letter to colonial government on the same day of the railway workers' threatened strike:

"Cost of native foodstuff has risen considerably since it was ruled that no maximum price could be fixed in view of the Prices of Goods Ordinance. The rise in the cost of native female clothing has risen approximately 100 p.c. and has caused dissatisfaction both in DSM and up-country. The Economic Control Board states that it has not been possible to fix the price of piece goods."[456]

On the same day the Labour Officer, Dar es Salaam, informed the Provincial Commissioner about the working conditions in the workshops:

"Railways Local Service - Part I.[...] Scales Shs. 60x3x72 p.m.; 76x4x100 p.m.; 105x5x130 p.m. Number of appointments in these scales is limited. Normal yearly increments - promotion above Shs 130/- are dependent on a knowledge of English.[...]

---

[455] LO, DSM, Report No. 20/4; 27/09/1941; TNA/S/R/ 30271.
[456] Provincer, Eastern Province, to Chief Sec., Dec. 19, 1941; TNA/S/R/ 30271.

Railways Local Service - Part II

(1) Monthly Contracts - comprising more reliable men based on attendance; estimated proportion so employed 40 p.c. to 50 p.c.

(a) skilled: Grades Shs.30, 35, 40, 45, 50, 55

(b) semi-skilled:

aa. Grade A: 30, 35, 40

bb. Grade B: 24 with grade steps of Sh.1 increases up to maximum of Shs. 29.

(2) Daily Contracts - paid at end of month for number of days worked during the month. Skilled, semi-skilled, unskilled: conversion rate of monthly wages to nearest 5 cts from minimum of Shs.21 to Shs 130. Wages of all employees on monthly and daily rates reviewed at end of the year, and promotion to higher grade dependent on efficiency and attendance, also that from daily to monthly contracts. Employees on monthly rates get better leave privileges than those on daily rates. Similarly those to whom Part I applies get better privileges than those under Part II.

C. Overtime

Weekdays: 6.30 - noon; 1 - 4 p.m. (equals) 8½ hours;

Saturdays: 6.30 - noon (equals) 5½ hours;

Overtime calculated at 1/32 daily rate for each ¬ hour worked. Normal overtime worked is 2 hours, making 10 hour shift. At present work continue to 4 p.m. on Saturdays and on Sundays from 7 p.m. to noon. Overtime is given in certain shops as far as possible to alternate shifts, and night shifts are interchanged every week with day shifts, to even out the overtime. Estimated that in certain shops employees are now working 40 hours per month overtime.

D. Night Shifts

4 p.m. to midnight with unofficial break of ½ hour at 8 p.m. No work after midnight, save perhaps for crane drivers on wharf. No employees are worked on day and night shifts continuously.

E. Approximate Number of African Employees (20/5/1941)

RLS Part I	RLS Part II	Apprentices
monthly	daily	
sk. ssk. unsk.	sk. ssk. unsk.[457]	
99 39 79	76 11 121	22".[458]

---

[457] 'sk.' denotes skilled worker; 'ssk.' semi-skilled, and 'unsk.' unskilled.
[458] LO, DSM, to Provincer, Eastern Province, Dec.19, 1941; TNA/S/R/ 30271.

This information conditioned the Labour Board that met for two days in Dar es Salaam in late January 1942.[459] The District Commissioner who represented the workers summarised the complaints and added that "unsympathetic handling of the workmen by superior officers; the daily contract system offers no securities of employment"[460] were further elements of complaints. The discussion focused on the adequate pay level and the basic costs of material reproduction. The District Officer tabled the cost of living index calculation that showed that present wage levels at the Railways were too low to cover the most basic reproduction:

"Cost of living index calculation: index 1 for the man and .83 for his wife, as used in the calculation of dietary scales in English social investigations.[...] Feeding: 3,754 calories pd. is sufficient for a sisal cutter or factory boy according to Medical Pamphlet No.29 (2nd ed.). It was found that this feeding based on the prices obtained on 19-9-1941 as published in General Notice No.863 of 1941 would cost per man cents 32.75 pd. on a maize staple and cents 40.25 on a rice staple with an average of cents 36.50 pd. , e.g. Shs.10.95 p.m. If wife is added total costs /amount/ to Shs.20.03 p.m..[...] 4. Clothing: Shs. 18/93; furniture, etc. not considered. The average minimum cost of living for a man and his wife without children in DSM as at 19th Sept. could be taken as Shs.40/-."[461]

The board members accepted this view. The problem was therefore how to meet this inescapably reasonable minimum under present industrial conditions. Food stuffs had risen by some 20 per cent,[462] and clothing by more than 100 per cent.[463]

---

[459] The Board's terms of reference: "To inquire into the causes of the recent dissatisfaction among native labour employed in the Railway Locomotive Workshops, Dar es Salaam, and to submit recommendations in this respect"; Memorandum for the Panel of the Labour Board Appointed To Inquire Into The Recent Dissatisfaction Among Certain Railway Employees in Dar ES Salaam; TNA/S/R/ 30271.
[460] Memorandum addressed to a Labour Board by the District Commissioner, Dar es Salaam, on behalf of the labour employed by the Chief Mechanical Engineer's Department of the Tanganyika Railways - January, 1942; TNA/S/R/ 30271.
[461] Minutes of Meeting of a Panel appointed from members of the Labour Board held at Dar es Salaam, Jan.23-24, 1942; approved March 2, 1942; TNA/S/R/ 30271, and Memorandum addressed to a Labour Board by the District Commissioner... January, 1942; TNA/S/R/ 30271.
[462] Average Retail Price in cents per lb.

Year	Maize	Millet (Mtama)	Rice	Groundnuts	Cassava (Muhogo)
1939	0.04	0.06	0.13-0.15	0.13	0.06
1941	0.06	0.06	0.16-0.18	0.19	0.06
1942	0.063	0.07	0.225		0.05

Sources: Tanganyika Territory, Blue Book, 1939, p.193; 1941, p.228; 1942, p.224.
[463] Comparative prices of clothing articles, 1939 and 1942 in Shs.

Item	1939	1942	Change
Kaniki, 2 pieces	2- 2/50	5- 5/50	150%

The panel recommended that wage adjustment only applied to workers who received a monthly wage below Shs.60.

According to the composition of staff the wage rise would affect some 400 workers: [464]

Africans under RLS (Part I):
457 over the whole system of which 159 are clerical or station staff; 298 Artisans and Locomotive Department staff; of this later, some 250 worked in DSM all at a rate of Shs.60 p.m. or over.

Africans under RLS (Part II):
6,000 to 7,000 of who some 600 work in DSM and of these some 370 in the Locomotive Shops for wages varying from Shs.21 to Shs.60 p.m..

The board agreed that the gap between lower wage rates and the cost of living should be bridged. This, however, should not be done by payment of a cash increase of wages or a cost of living allowance but by the issue of rations to the labourers, those who draw a monthly wage below Shs.60. This approach seemed reasonable as "[a] cash increase would have widespread repercussions and further, if considerably higher wages were to paid in DSM as a consequence there would be a danger of an increased migration to the town which was undesirable. Rations should be based on the model diet of Medical Pamphlet No. 29. It would cost at present rates, if purchased in bulk, about Shs.6/- for each man. If bought individually at retail prices: Shs.11/-. By this arrangement of rationing the earnings of the worker would in fact be increased by Shs.11/- while the actual cost to Government would be about Shs.6/-."[465]

Moreover, the board recommended a full investigation into social conditions of youth employed at Shs.5 to Shs.6 a month. This youth "came from outside the town and [...] also to such matters as the institution of eating houses, sleeping houses, the control of immigration into the townships and a survey of the difficulties of native

Kangas	2/50- 3	6- 7	140%
Shorts	1/50- 2/50	3/50	130%
Blankets	2	5- 6	150%

Source: Memorandum addressed to a Labour Board by the District Commissioner... January, 1942; TNA/S/R/ 30271.
[464] Minutes of Meeting... Jan.23-24, 1942; TNA/S/R/ 30271.
[465] Minutes of Meeting... Jan.23-24, 1942; TNA/S/R/ 30271.

life in DSM. Arrangements had already been made to station a Labour Officer in DSM for township work who would also deal with general welfare questions."[466]

The Panel Report was submitted on 3 March 1942, and approved.[467] Eventually, the workers were successful. But, this comprises did not contain a solid solution. Cash wages remained unchanged what in combination with uncontrolled inflation pointed towards new conflicts. It must be kept in mind that the action of December 1941 had been launched by the skilled, permanent African staff that was excluded from wage adjustments. Also, the unskilled, casual labour could not be satisfied with the outcome precisely as reproduction remained precarious and insecure. The Railways, the other antagonist in the struggle, preserved the non-comprising attitude for future conflicts. This is documented in the internal assessment report by the General Manager in the aftermath of the labour conflict:

"It was essential to introduce just staff conditions if labour troubles and strikes are to be avoided.[...] Fixation of wages rates:

(a) Asian staff were originally employed in Tanganyika on the conditions which would prove sufficiently attractive for them to leave India. The position is now changing rapidly. Since 1931 no Asian staff have been recruited from India but locally domiciled Asians have been engaged on RLS terms;

(b) Africans are now to an increasing extent taking the place of Asians both as clerks or artisans, such Africans are inclined to consider that they should be paid at the rates previously paid to Asians when they perform (or think they are performing) work which was previously done by Asians. The Management has strong views that the rates of pay to be given to all employees in the Railways L.S. (whether such employees are Africans or not) must be based solely on the economy of Tanganyika and not on rates (now largely conventional) based on conditions prevailing in India or else-where;

(c) Estimate: national income of Tanganyika at £10 mn p.a. or approximately £2 per head or £8 per male of working age. It is considered that until the lot of those large numbers earning less than this average can be improved ... the rising of higher wage rates should be handled with great caution".[468]

---

[466] Minutes of Meeting... Jan.23-24, 1942; TNA/S/R/ 30271.
[467] TNA/S/R/S.M.P. 30271.
[468] Review by GMR regarding conditions applied to Railway Staff on daily rates and monthly paid staff earning less than Shs 6o/- p.m.; TNA/S/R/ 30271.

This report outlined the substitution of Indians by African labour whose advance would save costs for the Railways. Also, Railways maintained the staff policy of individual, arbitrary progress as the General Manager had explained to the Labour Board.[469] As this policy had, in principle, been adopted since the mid-twenties it must be concluded that Railways cemented its attitude irrespective of changing conditions. How uncompromising the Railways Administration was is documented by the following letter in which the newly appointed General Manager outlined his policy:
"Labour conditions in Tanganyika were inferior to Kenya:
(a) a larger proportion of permanent labour employed on daily contract had no privileges whatsoever;
(b) the lack of any means of awarding gratuities to non-contributors to the Provident Fund who had served for long periods but had reached the end of their useful working life.
2. The change from monthly rates to daily rates had been effected within the few years previous to my arrival 'as a measure of economy'. It should be remembered that the Railways had an accrued deficit of almost £250,000, had made no provisions for depreciation and were then operating at a deficit and I was charged with ensuring that if at all possible the railway did not become a liability to the Territory and an additional burden on the taxpayers of the Territory. For this reason alone I could not, in justice to the railway users and the taxpayers, indulge in any great or rapid improvement in labour conditions. During the last 3 years I have had an examination made of the workings of the chief departments with two particular aims:
(a) to reduce the numbers of the staff on daily contracts;
(b) to improve the lot of those left on daily rates.
3. Wage level:
(a) as a whole the total amount of wages paid to manual workers can only be increased if the total values of production is increased;
(b) Railways comply with the so-called "District" rates, and no difficulty is experienced in obtaining workers at these rates. Generally it is in the interests of the railway to give steady employment to its employees and thus attract the better men from the

---

[469] "Promotion [...] achieved purely by selection according to GMR. A bar to the advancement of men from Part II is lack of efficiency but here a complaint may arise from the fact that it is the foremen who make recommendations for promotion"; Minutes of Meeting... Jan.23-24, 1942; TNA/S/R/ 30271.

labour market and I therefore favour rates being functionally higher (say about 10%) than the ruling rates so that the best men available may be obtained."[470]

Against this background it was no surprise that new strikes occurred. At Mwanza, the wharf labour of the Railway Administration went on strike in late 1942. The dissatisfaction was caused by low pay rates and long hours of work. In consequence, the number of permanent wharf workers increased, hereby reducing the working hours; at the same time, pay rates were adjusted from Shs.16 to Shs.22 per month.[471] Less than ten months later, the Dar es Salaam dockworkers went on strike that lasted for 10 days. Eight hundred men including much permanent staff, all registered casual labour complained about the existing economic conditions. The findings of the Labour Tribunal established on the fifth day of the strike under Defence (Trade Disputes) Regulations[472] confirmed that "strike had its origin in the labour's gathering discontent with the reduced value of their existing wages arising from the greatly increased cost of living, and that this discontent came to a head in an entirely natural way, being no doubt assisted in the process by the grant of a cost of living bonus to their fellow-Africans in Government service a few weeks before".[473] Colonial government submitted to the pressure; uplifted the wage rates; introduced a bonus system, and issued rations. These measures became effective for the whole colony.[474]

However, wage rise fell short of the increase of living costs of not less than fifty per cent since 1939, according to the Cost of Living Relief Committee.[475] Thus, new conflicts were unavoidable. Again, the same pattern prevailed. Colonial government compromised when put under pressure; the material concessions did not meet the expectations whereby the seeds for the next conflicts were sown. Apparently, colonial authorities lost control and became the reactive part in these struggles whose course was gradually dictated by the African workers.

---

[470] GMR to Lab. Com., DSM, April 2, 1940 (3518, confidential); TNA/S/R/ 30271.
[471] Labour Department, Annual Report, 1942, p.6.
[472] Government Notice No.279/1943.
[473] Labour Department, Annual Report, 1943, p.7.
[474] Labour Department, Annual Report, 1943, pp.7-8.
[475] Findings according to Labour Department, Annual Report, 1943, p.7.

IV.

The rapid change from indifference towards action was propelled by the material hardships, the lack of progress, and insecurity at the workplace. Because of early successes in these conflicts, self-consciousness rose that translated into a new social identity. As neither of the urging factors had been elevated new forms of organised protest had to be looked after.

The strikes of 1937 and 1939 were backward-looking and defensive actions demanding the restoration of the wage levels that had existed before the economic depression. The next strike in August 1943 had been carried by permanent workers; it revealed the dockworkers' organisation weakness for the colonial authorities dismissed the leading workers whom the strikers could not protect.[476]

The formation of trade unions and labour associations promised the alternative against former spontaneous actions and protection against the employers' display of power. By 1945, the Railway African Association was the most powerful workers' organisation in the colony with some 2,000 members.[477] How it was founded, how it was organised, what role in played in disputes cannot be answered. But, it became the eminent factor in the general strike of 1947. From this well-documented case some of the answers will be found.

After 8 May 1945, a new constellation appeared. The war economy had created massive employment schemes that became redundant as the economy adjusted to post-war demands. Thus, unemployment was a new social phenomenon that carried new conflicts. Also, the colonial power pressed for rural modernisation that would jeopardise the linkages between temporary labour and the return to the land; the only means of material protection in the old age. Finally, the war economy had accelerated urbanisation; the population of Dar es Salaam roughly doubled during the war while housing and infrastructure failed to cope with the rising demand. The already dreadful social situation deteriorated even further.[478]

These factors explain the militancy through which daily workers and casuals struggled for permanent employment and social security. Permanent labour, the

---

[476] Iliffe, Modern History of Tanganyika, pp.401f; for an account of this strike see Iliffe, 'The Creation of Group Consciousness Among the Dockworkers of Dar es Salaam', pp.58-61.
[477] Labour Department, Annual Report, 1945, p.11; Iliffe, Modern History of Tanganyika, p.397.
[478] Iliffe, 'The Creation of Group Consciousness Among the Dockworkers of Dar es Salaam', p.61.

most advanced social group, having already gained these advantages, found itself exposed to material decline. Irrespective of the social position within the colonial hierarchy, Tanganyika's wage labour force was prepared to struggling for structural improvement.

The 'uncaptured work force' faced a colonial power in search of a new policy. The Labour Party in power envisioned a more liberal colonial policy that it combined with economic development for the benefit of Britain's post-war reconstruction. This approach favoured the introduction of trade unions. It was expected that organised labour i) would facilitate economic planning; ii) would restrict the power of colonial capitalism; and iii) would correspond to Labour's ideological model.[479] The new social equilibrium, however, was doomed to failure because ultimately the ruling Labour Party adopted the subtle policy of social engineering that would benefit the interests of British industries. Social engineering related to the open disdain against social conditions *in situ* that were substituted from the universal model of trade unions. Also, the material side of Tanganyika's work force was neglected: wages were not adjusted to inflation,[480] and new employment schemes failed to turn up.[481] Thus, the factors of conflicts that had conditioned the war years persisted; meanwhile, the legalisation of trade unions had rendered labour an organisational strength that had lacked in the preceding struggles. For these reasons the next conflict would be more militant.

On 22 August 1947 the Dar es Salaam dockworkers informed the port companies "that unless considerable improvements were made in their wages and terms and conditions of service they would cease work at the end of the month".[482] Despite pressure from the Labour Department no firm offer was made until September 5 by which time the workers were resentful of the delay and eventually stopped work on the next day.[483] "Two days later the strike spread to other casual workers and some

---

[479] A. Gupta, *Imperialism and the British Labour Movement, 1914-1964*. London 1975, pp.275ff.
[480] According to Labour Department, Annual Report, 1947, p.20, there existed an "increasing resentment among the African working population against the continuous rise in living costs, coupled with the extreme difficulty in obtaining essential commodities at any price".
[481] Until September 1946 the demobilisation scheme was completed whereby approximately 91,000 African servicemen were discharged from the army. The Labour Exchange should help their integration in the civil economy. By December 1947, only 20,670 had been placed in employment; cf. Labour Department, Annual Report, 1946, p.20; 1947, p.11.
[482] Labour Department, Annual Report, 1947, p.21. The workers demanded a rise in the casual daily rate from Shs.2.30 to Shs.5, and a pay rate basis of Shs. 100 for permanent employees; Iliffe, 'The Creation of Group Consciousness Among the Dockworkers of Dar es Salaam', p.62.
[483] Employers offered "permanent workers increases of a few shillings a month and casual workers 20 cents more a day"; Iliffe, 'The Creation of Group Consciousness Among the Dockworkers of Dar es Salaam', p.62.

intimidation was reported".[484] The railway workers decided to join the strike. Because of the railway communication system information from Dar es Salaam rapidly reached the inland towns of Morogoro, Dodoma, Tabora, Kigoma, and Mwanza where railway staff joined the movement. Apparently, the same factors that propelled the Dar es Salaam workers applied to the rest of the work force in the colony.

By September 11, "Dar es Salaam was in ferment, with few Africans at work, pikketing throughout the town".[485] Official sources later admitted that the stoppage had been supported by all sections of the African population.[486] Colonial administration reacted vigorously by sending troops to Dar es Salaam and arresting 45 people and some were imprisoned for a year for intimidation. Also it broadcasted a stern warning to civil servants "to return to work under pain of instant dismissal".[487] On September 14 the mass meeting of the dockworkers was divided on continuing the strike, but that day the pickets at the port entrance gates were removed. The next day, more than seventy per cent of the dockers reported for work.[488]

In the rest of the colony, however, the general strike was only beginning. At Morogoro, the railway workers were joined by other urban workers and labour of the surrounding sisal plantations.[489] It ended on September 15 when the Dar es Salaam secretary of the Railways African Association instructed the local office to return to work. At Tabora, the Association demanded "Equal Pay For Equal Work". This request was supported from the local civil servants. In addition to wage increases they claimed the abolition of the colour bar at the work place: "We are now tired with these zigzag regulations of our Tanganyika Government, equal pay for equal work is not recognised and this can easily be seen from our present salaries which have entirely been based on racial prejudice. Up to this time African is serving absolutely under colour bar system".[490]

At Mwanza, dockworkers' militancy manifested itself in street fights. At the Uruwira lead mines in Mpanda the strike lasted until October 6.

By threat and concession colonial government succeeded in the mastering of the explosive situation. On the height of the strike, an Arbitration Tribunal was at once

---

[484] Iliffe, Modern History of Tanganyika, p.402.
[485] Iliffe, Modern History of Tanganyika, p.402.
[486] Labour Department, Annual Report, 1947, p.21.
[487] Labour Department, Annual Report, 1947, p.22.
[488] Iliffe, Modern History of Tanganyika, p.403.
[489] Labour Department, Annual Report, 1947, p.22.
[490] Document quoted in Iliffe, Modern History of Tanganyika, p.403.

set up "to inquire into the dispute in the port".[491] Explicitly on this reference, the so-called Hatchell Award was concluded. It resulted in the wage increase of c.30 per cent for dockworkers. Shortly after, wage rises in other sectors occurred. The colonial administration fixed minimum wage at Shs.41/50 per month. Casual labour was conceded a pay increase of 50 per cent with the minimum pay rate of Shs.1/60 per day.[492]

It seems that the African workers were triumphant; "[t]hey had defeated the employers before the hitherto hostile machinery of government."[493] The material gains and the right for organisation were won by the first real exercise of African power.[494] But, the strike exposed the limits of solidarity among workers. First, labour action was confined to the area along the Central line and its branches; second, government employees succumbed to pressure; third, joint action did not create a general trade union. What was created was the powerful trade union among the Dar es Salaam dockworkers[495] and other industrial branches. Nevertheless, the emergence of trade unions indicated the apogée rather than the apex of the Tanganyika labour movement.

Colonial administration accepted trade unions due to pressure of the Labour Party in power. Once organisation of labour was achieved it allowed for subtle, yet tight control through legal procedures, material support, and expertise by the British TUC.[496] Labour Department offered its support to the dockers' union on the ground that "[d]ockers had no experience of the administration side of union organisation".[497] Moreover, under this influence, the union struggled for the decasualisation of dockworkers and the creation of a more regular labour force.[498] Parallel to it, the union showed strong solidarity with labour grievances during 1948 and 1949.[499] While the

---

[491] Labour Department, Annual Report, 1947, p.22.
[492] Labour Department, Annual Report, 1947, p.17; Iliffe, 'The Creation of Group Consciousness Among the Dockworkers of Dar es Salaam', p.64.
[493] John Iliffe, 'A History of the Dockworkers of Dar es Salaam', in *Tanzania Notes and Records*, 71, 1970, p.133.
[494] Iliffe, 'A History of the Dockworkers of Dar es Salaam', p.134.
[495] Iliffe, Modern History of Tanganyika, p.404. By the end of 1947 the union claimed some 1,500 members, probably very nearly all the men regularly employed in the port; Iliffe, 'A History of the Dockworkers of Dar es Salaam', p.134
[496] According to the official history of TANU: *Historia Ya Chama Cha TANU 1954 Hadi 1977*. Dar es Salaam 1981, pp.15ff.
[497] Labour Department, Annual Report, 1949, p.27. Iliffe ('The Creation of Group Consciousness Among the Dockworkers of Dar es Salaam', p.65) argues that government presented with a powerful body decided to try to direct it into 'constructive' channels with the help from the Labour Department.
[498] Shivji, Law, State, and the Working Class, p.174; Iliffe, 'The Creation of Group Consciousness Among the Dockworkers of Dar es Salaam', pp.65-7.
[499] As inequality at wage level persisted the material side for workers' action was self-evident. According to an official survey in 1952 the number of regular employees amounted to c.350,000; of them 195,000 earned less

collaboration with the registration scheme strengthened the union's position it led to the exclusion of casual labour. When the latter group opposed this scheme[500] the strike on 31 January 1950, colonial administration intervened immediately by show of force and dispatched the King's African Rifles.[501] At the same time, blackleg labour was employed. The union's protest was met with arrests. Some 145 unionists were charged with offences about the strike.[502] Meanwhile, port work relied on 'volunteer' labour and those casual workers who had resumed work.[503] "But skilled permanent workers never returned, and with their departure the dock working class temporarily lost the heroic tradition of initiative and leadership".[504] The union was dissolved by a High Court order and the property confiscated by colonial government. This ended the collective organisation of African labour. Even worse because of the almost complete turnover of senior workers the traditions and experience that had been accumulated during the previous struggles were destroyed.[505]

Eventually, the colonial power restored its control after a period that had witnessed the rise of organised labour.[506] It took another five years before a territory-wide labour organisation was established[507] that adopted the British trade union model under advice from the Labour Department.[508] The Tanganyika Federation of Labour (TFL) linked its activities with the nationalist movement, Tanganyika African National Union (TANU). The nationalists' main objective was "to prepare the people of Tanganyika for self-government and Independence, and to fight relentlessly until Tanganyika is self-governing and independent".[509]

---

than Shs.40 per month; Labour Department, Annual Report, 1952, p.66, table III. The empirical evidence suggests that the vast majority lived in deep poverty.
[500] The port authorities and companies widened the scheme for control of the dockworkers with the intention "to gradually weed out the less regular workers and create a more efficient working force"; Labour Department, Annual Report, 1950, p.19.
[501] Because of "[i]ncreasing disillusionment within the colonial government with trade unionism in Tanganyika stemmed from the fact that the newly created Dockworkers Union was apparently not going to act in a 'reasonable British' manner" (William H. Friedland, *Vuta Kamba. The Development of Trade Unions in Tanganyika*. Stanford, 1969, p.36), the strike enabled the colonial authorities to solve this issue.
[502] For the accusations see Labour Department, Annual Report, 1950, p.18.
[503] On February 5, about 720 volunteers were employed; according to Labour Department, Annual Report, 1950, p.20 "labour supply was adequate for the normal functioning of the port".
[504] Shivji, Law, State, and the Working Class, p.175. But the employers profited from the new situation as productivity, measured in average tonnage handled per man-month, increased from 3 tons in 1949 to 6.76 tons in 1951; Labour Department, Annual Report, 1951, p.7.
[505] Iliffe, 'The Creation of Group Consciousness Among the Dockworkers of Dar es Salaam', p.69.
[506] The Labour Officer who had advised the dockworkers union told employers in Tanga that "Government were of the opinion that the African was at the present time quite unable to accept responsibility in a Trade Union sense"; Minutes of a meeting, Tanga, April 28, 1950; Labour Department 126/4/3.
[507] The weakness of organised labour was not lost on colonial capitalism as the number of casual labour increased from 27,703 in 1949 to 64,992 in 1951 while permanent labour was reduced by 50,000 over the same years; cf. Labour Department, Annual Report, 1951, p.8.
[508] Friedland, Vuta Kamba, pp.48-51.
[509] Henry Bienen, *Tanzania: Party Transformation and Economic Development*. Princeton 1970, p.29.

The foundation of TFL subordinated organised labour under the nationalist struggle. Adopting the British model, TFL gained support even from colonial administration; furthermore, the pre-dominance of the African *salariat* was evident that led to the specific constellation whereby manual labour was not adequately represented.[510] As the African civil servants were prohibited from joining TANU the trade unions constituted the only platform of political articulation. With the nationalist movement run by professional politicians a close co-operation ensued[511] that founded the nationalist pre-dominance over the labour movement.[512]

V.

In the broader perspective of the entire colonial society, the analysis of pre-independence nationalism would show how the urban-based political core owed rapid and spectacular successes to peasant pressure that frontally attacked colonialism's vital area. As containment failed the nationalist core exploited this strategic deficit in colonial politics without being firmly rooted in the peasant movements. In consequence, Tanganyika peasants became the decisive, yet voiceless vector in power politics.[513] On the one hand, the nationalist core neglected the promulgation of peasant positions in real terms while, on the other, the colonial state reproduced conflicts and contradictions in the rural arena.[514]

For the following reasons nationalism emerged as a usurping factor of the peasantry whereby the foundations of future failure in post-independence reconstruction were already anticipated.

---

[510] Iliffe, 'A History of the Dockworkers of Dar es Salaam', p.140. This is also evidenced by the post-1950 creation of trade unions whose "leadership, unlike that of the Dockworkers Union, came from westernized and educated clerks rather than from illiterate manual workers. Small unions began to appear which, under the guidance of the Labour Department, were localized and craft-based", Friedland, Vuta Kamba, p.21. Also, TFL was the central organisation of the affiliated trade unions at industrial levels. The activities were performed by professionals who held close links with the nationalist movement through which it could check colonial administration; cf. William H. Friedland, 'Co-operation, Conflict, and Conscription: TANU-TFL Relations, 1955-1964', in Jeffrey Butler and A.A. Castagno (ed.), *Boston University Papers in African Politics*. New York, 1967, pp.67-103.
[511] Organic link between the TFL and TANU took place in 1961; prior to that normalisation union leaders co-operated with TANU leaders on an individual basis with the approval from the members; Wogu Ananaba, *The Trade Union Movement in Africa. Promise and Performance*. London 1979, pp.34f.
[512] Friedland, Vuta Kamba, pp.21f.
[513] According to the 1950 census out of the African population of 7,590,000 less than 6 per cent, 444,000, classified as employees and workers; Labour Department, Annual Report, 1952, p.1.
[514] Colonial administration instructed all Provincial Commissioners "to induce the African to contribute, either directly or indirectly, to the economic wealth and development...producing ...something more than the crop of local foodstuffs that he requires for the sustenance of himself and his family on a static standard of living"; Government Circular No.1 of 1952; TNA/S/R/ S.M.P. 42152.

None of the peasant leaders was integrated into the leadership. Nationalism remained revealingly vague in new agrarian policy other than the rejection of colonial practice. The leadership deployed mass mobilisation as one tactical weapon with emphasis on diplomatic incentives. Furthermore, the leadership's position of bulkheading the nationalist ship off mass participation gave it credentials among the colonial power and facilitated the march towards independence.[515]

Eventually, the nationalist party portrayed the same patterns and structures as did western parties. The quest for power prevailed over demonopolisation, that is the delegation of power onto the social classes for which the political struggle was fought. Politics preserved the frontal and coercive approach - the historical constant factor that was to erode many prospects of genuine transformation.

---

[515] Bienen, Tanzania, p.40f.

8. Conclusion

The Railways neatly mirrors the policy of British colonialism in Tanganyika. Having acquired the former German colony for strategic reasons the new power administered the territory without incentives for development.

Similar to the other economic sectors the colonial power treated the Railways as one means for revenue extraction. This attitude conditioned the Railways as vehicle of cheap transport. It also explains the financial policy of 'credit peonage'. From the beginning, the Railways was undercapitalised what made loans vital. As these loans were linked to a strictly commercial conditionality the Railways' surplus went into debt service that ruled out any modernisation of infrastructure and equipment. The credit policy persisted throughout the general economic situation what forced the Railways to deep cost cuts primarily for the financial obligations. Finances give the first reason why the Railways failed to enhance economic development.

The second reason must be looked after the colonial policy. Instead of being reinvested in the colony surplus was absorbed by the colonial state. This transfer blocked development and enclosed the economy in structural backwardness that limited the demand for new railway lines.

Moreover, these reasons condition the operations of the Railways. Financial obligations forced the Railways into operational adjustment. Cost reductions in combination with productivity increases were constant factors in railway politics. As the activated resources mainly went into the debt service neither the material foundations at the work place nor the quality of staff improved. The Railways focused on labour-intensive works on the basis of cheap African labour and low investments in machinery and tools. Productivity increases followed from the reduction of the work force and the costs at the work place and not from investment.

The necessary flexibility combined rightlessness and poor pay. For this strategic objective the African work force was denied any form of organisation that would strengthen its bargaining power. The obvious disdain of work ethics as expressed by adequate pay, working hours, and condition at work site renders the Railways the features of the typical colonial enterprise. This pattern explains why workers' demands for adequate pay and job security were linked to strikes and spontaneous protests. These actions were not successful primarily for the social composition of the Railways staff that was dominated by casual and unskilled labour. Also, the colonial power intervened very sharply because the Railways was the largest employer in Tanganyika. Any concessions, in material terms and in workers' rights, would spread to the modern sector and could probably destabilise the colonial power's monopoly.

Denials of basic rights together with inadequate pay define the pattern of 'open exploitation'. It persisted throughout the twenties and thirties. The quest for modernisation started under the war economy and continued after the war. The modernisation strategy was based on state-centred planning and the regrouping of economic activities in East Africa. The regional co-operation favoured Kenya that emerged as the regional core economy with Uganda and Tanganyika as periphery. Thus, post-war modernisation created a new structure of underdevelopment that fostered Tanganyika's backwardness while improvements at sectoral level, that is industrialisation, were precluded as was the formation of an educated, technically skilled work force.

Eventually, the Railways served its infrastructure mission for British colonialism in Tanganyika that was a burden but not an asset in post-colonial reconstruction.

Bibliography

I. Documentary Sources

A. Tanzania National Archives, Dar es Salaam:

Secretarial File R. "Railways"

R.1	Railways, General	299 File Entries
(R.2	Railway Workshops	nil)
R.3	Engines and Rolling Stock	20 File Entries
R.4	Way and Works	12 File Entries
R.5	Passenger and Goods Rates	59 File Entries
R.6	Further Railway Construction	26 File Entries
R.7	Surveys	5 File Entries

B. University Liberary, East Africana Section, Dar es Salaam:

Armitage-Smith, Sidney. Report on a Financial Mission to Tanganyika, 26th September 1932. *Cmd 4182.* London, 1932.
Colonial Office. *Report by His Britannic Majesty's Government to the Council of the League of Nations on the Administration of Tanganyika Territory for the Year 1927.* London, 1927.
Deutsche Kolonial-Eisenbahn-Bau und Betriebsgesellschaft. *Von der Küste zum Kilimanjaro.* Berlin, n.d.
Jahrbuch über die deutschen Kolonien, 1, 1908; 2, 1909; 3, 1910; 5, 1912.
Koloniales Jahrbuch, 9,1897.
Kolonialpolitisches Aktionskomittee. *Die Eisenbahnen Afrikas. Grundlagen und Gesichtspunkte für eine koloniale Eisenbahnpolitik.* Berlin, 1907.
Reichskolonialamt. *Amtliche Jahresberichte. Die deutschen Schutzgebiete in Afrika und der Südsee 1909/10.* Berlin, 1910. (afterwards: Amtlicher Jahresbericht)
Report on Tanganyika Territory. Dar es Salaam, 1922 - 1938.
Secretary of State for the Colonies. Report of the East African Commission. *Cmd 2387.* London, 1925.
Secretary of State for the Colonies. *Report of the Railway System of Tanganyika Territory by Brigadier-General F.D. Hammond.* London, 1930.
Secretary of State for the Colonies. *Report on the Railway Systems of Kenya, Uganda and Tanganyika by Lieut.-Colonel F.D. Hammond.* London, 1921.
Tanganyika Railways. *(Acting) Traffic Manager Report.* Dar es Salaam, 1923 - 1939.
Tanganyika Railways. *Annual Report.* Dar es Salaam, 1921 - 1947.
Tanganyika Railways. *Chief Accountant Report.* Dar es Salaam, 1923 - 1939.
Tanganyika Railways. *Chief Mechanical Engineer Report.* Dar es Salaam, 1923 - 1939.
Tanganyika Railways. *General Manager Report.* Dar es Salaam, 1921 - 1947.
Tanganyika Territory. *Blue Book for the Year ended 31st December.* Dar es Salaam, 1922 - 1948.
Tanganyika Territory. *Labour Department Annual Report.* Dar es Salaam, 1927-1930; 1940 - 1952.
Tanganyika Territory. *Report of the Tanganyika Railway Commission.* London, 1930.
Tanganyika Territory. *Report on Preliminary Surveys to open up the South-West of Tanganyika by C. Gillman, Chief Engineer.* London 1929.
Tanganyika Territory. *Trade Report for 1921.* Dar es Salaam, 1921.
Tanganyika. *Report of the Commission Appointed to Enquire into the Disturbances which occurred in the Port of Tanga during the month of August 1939.* Dar es Salaam, 1939.
Tanganyika. *Revised Development and Welfare Plan for Tanganyika 1950-1956.* Dar es Salaam, 1951.
Tanganyika. Statistical Abstract 1938-1952. Dar es Salaam, 1954.

II. Other Works Cited

Ananaba, Wogu. *The Trade Union Movement in Africa. Promise and Performance.* London 1979.
Austen, Ralph A. *African Economic History. Internal Development and External Dependency.* London, 1987.
Bailey, Martin. *Freedom Railway. China and the Tanzania-Zambia Link.* London, 1976.
Balzer, F. *Die Kolonialbahnen mit besonderer Berücksichtigung Afrikas.* Berlin und Leipzig, 1916.
Bank of Tanzania, *Tanzania: Twenty Years of Independence (1961-1981). A Review of Political and Economic Performance.* Dar es Salaam, n.d..
Bates, Margaret L. 'Social Engineering, Multi-racialism, and the Rise of TANU: the Trust Territory of Tanganyika 1945-1961', in D.A. Low and Alison Smith (ed.), *History of East Africa.* Vol. III. Oxford, 1976.
Bates, Robert. *Essays on the Political Economy of Rural Africa.* Cambridge, 1982.
Beachey, R.W. 'East African Ivory Trade in the Nineteenth Century', *Journal of African History*, 2, 8, 1967.
Beer, G.L. *African Questions at the Paris Peace Conference wiith papers on Egypt, Mesopotamia, and the colonial settlement.* London, 1923.
Bennett, Norman R. 'Arab Impact', in Bethwell A. Ogot (ed.), *Zamani. A Survey of East African History.* Nairobi, 1974.
Bennett. *A History of the Arab State of Zanzibar.* London, 1978.
Bentwich, N. *The Mandates System.* London, 1930.
Bienen, Henry. *Tanzania: Party Transformation and Economic Development.* Princeton 1970.
Biermann, Werner. *Kolonie und City. Britische Wirtschaftsstrategie und -politik in Tanganyika, 1920-1955.* Saarbrücken und Fort Lauderdale, 1991.
Biermann, Werner. *Wachuurizi Na Halasa. Händler und Handelskapital in der wirtschaftlichen Entwicklung Ostafrikas (900 bis 1890).* Münster und Hamburg, 1993.
Bowles, B.D. 'The political economy of colonial Tanganyika 1939-1961', in M.H.Y. Kaniki (ed.), *Tanzania under Colonial Rule.* London, 1980.
Brett, Edward A. *Colonialism and Underdevelopment in East Africa. The politics of economic change 1919-1939.* London, 1973.
Brown, Beverly. 'Ujiji: The History of a Lakeside Town, c.1800-1914.' Ph.D.thesis, Boston University, 1973.
Büttner, Kurt. *Die Anfänge der deutschen Kolonialpolitik in Ostafrika. Eine kritische Untersuchung an Hand unveröffentlichter Quellen.* East Berlin, 1959.
Chidzero, Bernard T.G. *Tanganyika and International Trusteeship.* Oxford, 1961.
Clagett Taylor, J. *The Political Development of Tanganyika.* Stanford, 1963.
Cooper, Frederick. *From Slaves to Squatters. Plantation Labour and Agriculture in Zanzibar and Coastal Kenya, 1890-1925.* Nairobi, 1981.
Coulson, Andrew. *Tanzania. A political economy.* Oxford, 1982.
de Wilde, John C. *Experiences with Agricultural Development in Tropical Africa.* Vol. II. The Case Studies. Baltimore, 1967.
Dundas, Sir Charles. *African Crossroads.* London, 1955.
Eberlie, R.F. 'The German Achievement in East Africa', *Tanganyika Notes and Records*, 55, 1960.
Feis, Herbert. *Europe the World's Banker.* New Haven, 1930.
Flint, J. 'Zanzibar 1890-1950', in V. Harlow and E.M. Chilver (ed.), *History of East Africa.* Vol.II. Nairobi, 1982.
Frankel, Sally H. 'The Kongwa Experiment', *The Colonial Review*, 6, 8, 1950.
Frankel, Sally H. *Capital Investment in Africa.* London, 1938.
Friedland, William H. 'Co-operation, Conflict, and Conscription: TANU-TFL Relations, 1955-1964', in Jeffrey Butler and A.A. Castagno (ed.), *Boston University Papers in African Politics.* New York, 1967.
Friedland, William H. *Vuta Kamba. The Development of Trade Unions in Tanganyika.* Stanford, 1969.
Gann, L.H. 'Economic Development in Germany's African Empire, 1884-1914', in Peter Duignan and L.H. Gann (ed.), *Colonialism in Africa 1870-1960.* Volume Four. The Economics of Colonialism. Cambridge, 1975.
Gann, L.H. and P. Duignan, *The Rulers of German Africa, 1884-1914.* London, 1975.
Gardner, B. *German East. The Story of the First World War in East Africa.* London 1963.
Gillman, C. 'A Short History of the Tanganyika Railways', in *Tanganyika Notes and Records*, 13, 1942.
Glassman, J. 'Social Rebellion and Swahili Culture: The Response to German Conquest of the Northern Mrima, 1888-1890.' Ph.D.thesis, University of Wisconsin, 1988.
Graf von Schweritz, H.H. 'Bedarf Deutsch-Ostafrika jetzt einer Zentralbahn?', in *Koloniales Jahrbuch*, 9, 1897.
Graham, J.D. 'Indirect Rule: The Establishment of 'Chiefs' and 'Tribes' in Cameron's Tanganyika', in *Tanzania Notes and Records*, 27/28, 1976.
Gupta, A. *Imperialism and the British Labour Movement, 1914-1964.* London 1975.
Gwassa, G.C.K. 'The German intervention and African resistance in Tanzania', in I.N. Kimambo and A.J. Temu (ed.), *A history of Tanzania.* Nairobi, 1969.
Hallgarten, George W.F. *Imperialismus vor 1914. Die soziologischen Grundlagen der Außenpolitik europäischer Großmächte vor dem ersten Weltkrieg.* Zweiter Band. München, 1963.
Hallgarten, George W.F. *Imperialismus vor 1914. Die soziologischen Grundlagen der Außenpolitik europäischer Großmächte vor dem ersten Weltkrieg.* Erster Band, München, 1963.
Hatch, John. *Tanzania. A Profile.* London, 1972.
Henderson, W.O. 'German East Africa, 1884-1918', in V. Harlow and E.M. Chilver (ed.), *History of East Africa.* Vol.II. Nairobi, 1982.

Hill, M.F. *Permanent Way*. Vol II. The Story of the Tanganyika Railways. Nairobi, 1957.
Hill, Patricia J. *National Archives of Tanzania. Shelf List and Index to Secretariat Archives. Early Series (1919-1927)*. Dar es Salaam, February 1966.
Hitchcock, E. 'The East African Sisal Industry', in *Rhodesia and East Africa*, 1958.
Hodgkin, Thomas. *Nationalism in Colonial Africa*. London, 1956.
Hofmeier, Rolf. *Transport and Economic Development in Tanzania with particular reference to roads and road transport*. München, 1972.
Hoyle, B.S. 'Early Port Development in East Africa', *Tijdschrift voor Economische en Sociale Geograpfie*, LVIII, 1967.
Hyden, Goran. *Beyond Ujamaa in Tanzania. Underdevelopment and an Uncaptured Peasantry*. London, 1980.
Iliffe, John. 'A History of the Dockworkers of Dar es Salaam', in *Tanzania Notes and Records*, 71, 1970.
Iliffe, John. 'The Creation of Group Consciousness Among the Dockworkers of Dar es Salaam 1929-50', in Richard Sandbrook and Robin Cohen (ed.), *The Development of an African Working Class. Studies in Class Formation and Action*. London, 1975.
Iliffe, John. *A Modern History of Tanganyika*. Cambridge, 1979.
Iliffe, John. *Tanganyika Under German Rule 1905-1912*. Cambridge, 1969.
Ingham, Kenneth. 'Tanganyika: Slump and Short-term Governors, 1932-1945', V. Harlow and E.M. Chilver (ed.), *History of East Africa*. Vol. II. Nairobi, 1982.
Ingham, Kenneth. 'Tanganyika: The Mandate and Cameron, 1919-1931', in V. Harlow and E.M. Chilver (ed.), *History of East Africa*. Vol.II. Nairobi, 1982.
Ingham, Kenneth. *A History of East Africa*. London, 1965.
Jackson, R.D. 'Resistance to the German invasion', in Robert I. Rotberg and A.A. Mazrui (ed.), *Protest and Power in Black Africa*. New York, 1970.
Jahn, G.K. 'Rückblick auf die Fortschritte unserer kolonialen Entwicklung', in *Jahrbuch über die deutschen Kolonien*, 1, 1908.
Joelson, F.S. *Germany's claims to Colonies*. London, 1939.
Kiernan, J.A. 'Abushiri and the Germans', *Hadith 2*, 1970.
Kim, Kwan S. et al. (ed.), *Papers on the Political Economy of Tanzania*. Nairobi, 1979.
Kirchhoff, D. 'Die Eisenbahnen im östlichen Kongostaat', in *Zeitschrift für Kolonialpolitik, Kolonialrecht und Kolonialwirtschaft*, 9. 1907.
Leubuscher, Christine. *Tanganyika Territory. A Study of Economic Policy under Mandate*. Oxford, 1944.
Leverett, C.W. 'An Outline of the History of Railways in Tanganyika', in *Tanganyika Notes and Records*, 46, 1957.
Lionel and John S. Saul (ed.), *Socialism in Tanzania. An Interdisciplinary Reader. Vol.1 Politics. Vol. 2 Policies*. Nairobi, 1973.
Listowel, Judith. *The Making of Tanganyika*. London, 1965.
Lloyd, T.O. *The British Empire 1558-1983*. London, 1984.
Lonsdale, John. 'Some Origins of Nationalism in Tanzania', in Lionel Cliffe and John S. Saul (ed.), *Socialism in Tanzania. An Interdisciplinary Reader. Vol.1 Politics*. Nairobi, 1973.
Lord Hailey, *An African Survey. A Study of Problems Arising in Africa South of the Sahara*. Revised 1956. Oxford, 1957.
Low, D.A. and Alison Smith (ed.), *History of East Africa*. Vol. III. Oxford, 1976.
Lumley, E.K. *Forgotten Mandate. A British District Officer in Tanganyika*. London, 1976.
Luxemburg, Rosa. *Die Akkumulation des Kapitals. Ein Beitrag zur ökonomischen Erklärung des Imperialismus*. Archiv sozialistischer Literatur 1. Frankfurt, 1966.
Maguire, G.A. *Toward 'Uhuru' in Tanzania. The Politics of Participation*. Cambridge, 1969.
Moffett, J.P., J.F.R. Hill. *Tanganyika: A Review of Its Resources and Their Development*. Dar es Salaam, 1955.
Morgan, Kenneth O. *Labour in Power 1945-1951*. Oxford, 1984.
Morris-Hale, W. 'British Administration in Tanganyika from 1920 to 1945 with special reference to the Preparation of Africans for Administration Positions'. Thèse, University of Geneva, 1969.
Most, K. *Die wirtschaftliche Entwicklung Deutsch-Ostafrikas, 1885-1905*. Berlin, 1905.
Mwansasu, Bismarck U. and Cranford Pratt (ed.), *Towards Socialism in Tanzania*. Dar es Salaam, 1979.
Pakenham, Thomas. *The Scramble for Africa 1876-1912*. London, 1991.
Pierand, R.V. 'The Dernburg Reform Policy and German East Africa', in *Tanzania Notes and Records*, 67, 1967.
Randzio, E. und K. Remy. *Kolonialbahnen. Die Koloniale Verkehrspolitik in Afrika*. Berlin, 1942.
Ranger, T.O. 'The movement of ideas, 1850-1939', in I.N. Kimambo and A.J. Temu (ed.), *A history of Tanzania*. Nairobi, 1969.
Rathenau, Walter. 'Erwägungen über die Erschließung des Deutsch-Ost-afrikanischen Schutzgebietes'. (1907) in *Nachgelassene Schriften*. Band II. Berlin, 1928.
Robbins, Michael. *The Railway Age*. London, 1962.
Rodney, Walter. 'The political economy of Tanganyika 1890-1930', in M.H.Y. Kaniki (ed.), *Tanzania under Colonial Rule*. London, 1980.
Rothschild, D.S. *Towards Unity in Africa: A Study of Federalism in British Africa*. Washington, D.C., 1960.
Schroeter, H. *Die Eisenbahnen der ehemaligen deutschen Schutzgebiete*. Frankfurt, 1961.
Shivji, Issa G. *Law, State and the Working Class in Tanzania c.1920-1964*. London, 1986.
Stahl, K.M. *The Metropolitan Organization of British Colonial Trade. Four Regional Studies*. London, 1951.
Steer, G.L. *Judgment on German Africa*. London, 1939.

Stephens, H.W. *The Political Transformation of Tanganyika: 1920-67.* New York, 1968.
Tambila, Kapepwa. 'A Plantation Labour Magnet: The Tanga Case', in Walter Rodney, K. Tambila, L. Sago, *Migrant Labour in Tanzania during the Colonial Period. Case Studies of Recruitment and Conditions of Labour in the Sisal Industry.* Hamburg, 1983.
TANU. *Historia Ya Chama Cha TANU 1954 Hadi 1977.* Dar es Salaam 1981.
Tetzlaff, Rainer. *Koloniale Entwicklung und Ausbeutung. Wirtschafts- und Sozialgeschichte Deutsch-Ostafrikas 1885-1914.* Berlin, 1970.
Thornton, A.P. *Imperialism in the Twentieth Century.* London, 1980.
Twining, Edward. 'The last nine years in Tanganyika', *African Affairs*, 50, 201, 1959.
von Bülow, H. *Deutschlands Kolonien und Kolonialkriege.* Leipzig, 1900.
von Sperber, K.W. *Public Administration in Tanzania.* München, 1970.
Waldmann, J. *Usambara railway construction.* Oxford, 1956.
Wehler, H.Ulrich. *Bismarck und der Imperialismus.* Köln, 1972.
Westcott, N.J. 'The Impact of the Second World War on Tanganyika, 1939-1949'. Ph.D.thesis, Cambridge University, 1982.
Wettich, H. *Die Entwicklung Usambaras unter Einfluß der ostafrikanischen Nordbahn.* Leipzig, 1911.
Williams, Gavin. 'Taking the Part of the Peasants: Rural Development in Nigeria and Tanzania', in Peter Gutkind and I. Wallerstein (ed.), *The Political Economy of Contemporary Africa.* Beverly Hills, 1976.
Wilson, Charles. 'The Economic Role And Mainsprings Of Imperialism', in Peter Duignan and L.H. Gann (ed.), *Colonialism in Africa 1870-1960.* Volume Four. The Economics of Colonialism. Cambridge, 1975.
Wood, A. *The Groundnut Affair.* London, 1950.
Wright, Marcia. *Report on the National Archives.* Dar es Salaam, 1962.
Zimmermann, E. *Die ostafrikanische Zentralbahn, der Tanganyikaverkehr und die ostafrikanischen Finanzen.* Berlin, 1911.

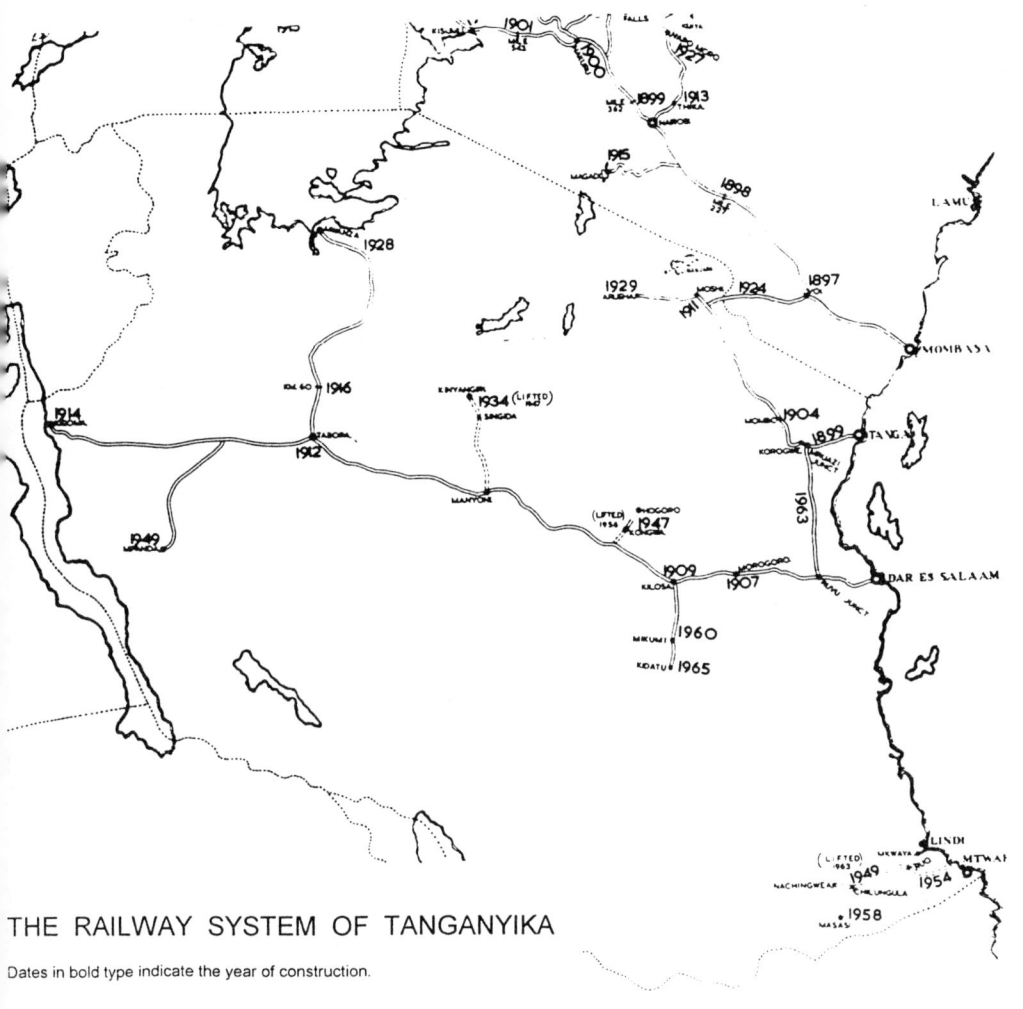

THE RAILWAY SYSTEM OF TANGANYIKA

Dates in bold type indicate the year of construction.